HOUDINI'S BOX

HOUDINI'S BOX

THE ART OF ESCAPE

Adam Phillips

PANTHEON BOOKS

NEW YORK

Grateful acknowledgment is made to the following for
permission to reprint previously published material:
HARPERCOLLINS PUBLISHERS, INC.: Excerpts from
Houdini!!! The Career of Eric Weiss by Kenneth Silverman.
Copyright © 1996 by Kenneth Silverman. Reprinted
by permission of HarperCollins Publishers, Inc.
HARVARD UNIVERSITY PRESS: Poem 144 and Poem 1364 from
The Poems of Emily Dickinson edited by Ralph W. Franklin
(Cambridge, Mass.: The Belknap Press of Harvard University
Press, Copyright © 1998 by the President and Fellows of Harvard
College). Copyright © 1951, 1955, 1979 by the President and
Fellows of Harvard College. Reprinted by permission of
Harvard University Press and the Trustees of Amherst College.

Library of Congress Cataloging-in-Publication Data

Phillips, Adam.
Houdini's box : the art of escape / Adam Phillips.
p.   cm.
Includes bibliographical references.
ISBN 0-375-40636-0
1. Escape (Psychology)   2. Escape (Ethics)
3. Conduct of life.   I. Title.
BF575.E83 P45   2001
128—dc21   00-050181

www.pantheonbooks.com

Book design by Cassandra J. Pappas

Printed in the United States of America
First Edition
2 4 6 8 9 7 5 3 1

for Clive Panto

The way to solve the problem you see in life is to live in a way that makes the problem disappear.

—Ludwig Wittgenstein,
Culture and Value

My sole concern was to borrow forms, no matter from where, by which my own preoccupations could declare themselves.

—Marion Milner,
An Experiment with Leisure

They desire to be good and bad at the same time.

—Sandor Lorand,
Compulsion Neurosis

HOUDINI'S BOX

A FIVE-YEAR-OLD GIRL comes into my room ready to play another round of her favorite game, hide-and-seek, a game she has been playing with me twice a week for several months. It is the way, down to the smallest detail, we always begin our time together. In the room there is an armchair, a table, and a chair. She stands in the middle of the room, closes her eyes, and says, "Start looking."

I have watched her, as usual, walk into the room and simply close her eyes. But in her mind she is now hiding. And quite quickly getting impatient.

"Look!" she says. "Start looking!" Of course I am looking—what else could I be doing?—but I don't seem to be playing the game. It occurs to me, for once, that perhaps *I* should close my eyes, which I do. And then she

3

says a bit crossly, "OK, I'll give you a clue. I'm not behind the chair."

I say to her, not too plaintively, "How will I ever find you?"

"Just keep looking," she says blithely, clearly wanting to be helpful. Then, a bit more frantic, a bit more Alice in Wonderland, "I can't escape, I can't escape . . . I must be here somewhere."

"No one can look everywhere," I say.

"We can't escape, we're doing that," she replies thoughtfully, as though this was the most sensible, least histrionic of acknowledgments.

She waits, eyes squeezed, while I keep failing to do what it looks like I've already done. So what I have found—indeed can't help seeing: her in the middle of the room, hiding—is obviously not what she wants me to look for.

"Will it be dangeroos when I find you?" I ask. (Her mother would read the sign at the zoo as "Do not feed these animals, they are dangeroos," so "dangeroos" is her word for it.)

"You'll die," she replies. Then there's a pause, and she says in her most world-weary voice, "I give up." And it is as if the rehearsal is over, and we can now resume, after another failed attempt at something, our ordinary life in the room.

There is a drama, a tableau that she has to show me, that we are both trapped in. This is what we have to take for granted, she seems to be saying, this is what we need to do together, to get things started. And the sign of our entrapment is that she never changes; whatever I say, her lines are always the same. So what I say—even though it is as different as I can make it each time, even though I rack my brains for what she wants to hear—seems equally repetitious. I am her desperate improviser, trying to spring her. I will only know if I am someone else to her if she wants to change her tune. But in this strange duet for one the hide-and-seek is like a dream game, secluded away; a play within a play that we both briefly enact and watch, and then give up on. She rarely refers to it afterwards, and I refer to it as much as I can, trying to fit it in or link it with the rest of her life. But because there is no conversation about it, because it is at once open and unopened, it is, to all intents and purposes, an unspoken thing between us.

I thought sometimes that there was a note of triumphant relief in her apparent dismay inside the game. She wants me to find her, but she warns me that I will suffer if I do; or she fears that no one really wants to find her because they wouldn't be able to bear the consequences. Either she is practicing her privacy or there is a solitude she feels imprisoned by. The girl standing in the middle of the room with her eyes closed sometimes seems to be parading her safety, and sometimes alerting us to a terror (people often feel most alive while they are escaping, most paralyzed before and after). But either way, what is most striking about the game, when we are playing it, is that I can't escape from looking for her, and she can't escape from hiding. There is nowhere else for either of us to go.

This girl has been referred to me for what is called, in the strange language of what is called Social Services, "query child sexual abuse," and truanting from home and school. So the voices of my (psychoanalytic) education provide me with a serviceable understanding of this apparently split-off game. There is something eerie about her ability to remember her lines—her knack of keeping them identical, whatever I say—but this too might be a way of managing a bewildering invasion (the violent imposition of another's desire making her mechanical). The game might literally repeat her experience: the impossibility of being able to hide, and the wish for a magical solution to this—all you have to do is close your eyes. If I do find her she fears that I will do something terrible to her—but the terror of waiting seems more unbearable than the terror of the event—or that she might do something to me. So I might think of myself as finding words for her fears, voicing what there might be to escape from, and one way or another providing reassurances about safety. But both she and I, in her "game" and my practice, are telling each other stories about safety and danger. Indeed, what else could there be to talk about? Whether or not fear is our founding passion, we are haunted by a picture of ourselves in flight, on the run. Whether we are getting away *from* something or getting away *with* something; as Icarus or Oedipus or Narcissus, as victims or tyrants, we cannot describe ourselves without also describing what we need to escape from, and what we believe we need to escape to.

When children play hide-and-seek—or when adults

are knowingly or unknowingly elusive with each other, playing at repulsion and enticement—what is being played with is the fear (and the wish) of never being found. When the game goes on too long the child who is hiding always helps the seeker out. No one must disappear for too long, no one must get too far away. And the odd moment of being found is the end of the game. But if playing hide-and-seek is one of our emblematic games— at once testing the appetite of the seeker and the resolve of the one who hides—it is also a game haunted by the possibility of escape, of being able to escape the intention, the desire of another (chosen) person. Every successful game of hide-and-seek—and one way or another, barring tragedy, it is always successful—reassures the players that no one can escape, that there is nowhere else to escape to. The transgression is to disappear, to find a place where no one keeps an eye on you. The puzzle of hide-and-seek— its absurd drama of conflicting wishes, in which to be found is to lose the game, and not being found has to be got just right—becomes a blueprint for the dilemma of the erotic, of whether we want our sexuality to inten- sify our self-consciousness or release us from it. In her game the little girl is convinced that neither of us can escape, that what we are doing is not escaping; that the adult is as confined as she is. What they (we) share is being trapped in something together, which might be called need or sexuality, or the wish for certain kinds of recogni- tion and reassurance.

When I first discussed this game with her parents, they told me that when she played hide-and-seek with her friends, "she often goes so far away that she's not really playing the game anymore." This had made her friends very scared at first, but eventually they got used to it and "didn't waste much time on her. . . . They don't bother." Beyond a certain point, after an uncertain amount of time, she has changed the game (and it is worth wondering what this particular kind of arranged solitude releases her into). And the impatience of her parents and her friends—verging on indifference, as impatience always does—seems to be an essential part of her drama, a message carefully though unconsciously sent, a reminder of the frustration that is afoot here. She makes everyone so impatient with her that they are quite unable to think exactly what it is that they are impatient for. Her not playing the game properly is not seen by her friends as a fascinating innovation; from their point of view she contributes nothing. But what do they want from her? What is assumed not to be working properly here, or indeed, in her? Like all so-called symptoms her truancy stages a dilemma for everyone involved with her. She creates a conflict inside them that they dispose of as blame and accusation. When she gets away—when the school, her friends, or her parents give up on her, that is, do the opposite of invade her—who is disappointing whom? Her behavior conjures up in people something they want to get rid of. It is not clear, when her friends just stop looking for her, who is fleeing from whom (or from what). To escape—or, of course, to be unable to escape—is often linked to a sense of failure.

Because it is apparently the preferred life one is escaping to, our fears are the key to our ideals. What we want is born of what we want to get away from. "She's a right little Houdini," her father told me, "she can't wait for anything."

HARRY HOUDINI, the great escapologist, was the son of a failed rabbi. And Houdini was not his real name. Born in Budapest in 1874—a year after the great Hungarian psychoanalyst Sándor Ferenczi—Erik Weisz was the third son of Rabbi Mayer Samuel Weiss, as his name was spelled when he arrived in America in 1876. A scholarly man, also trained in the law, Rabbi Weiss failed to establish himself in an America that was becoming the main destination for the growing exodus of European Jews (in the 1880s over 200,000 eastern European Jews arrived in New York alone). Houdini's father came to America by himself; his family joined him in 1878 for what was to become sixteen years of itinerant failure. Unable to establish himself as a rabbi in Wisconsin or New York, he ended up working as a cutter in a ready-made clothing business in New York, where Erik as a teenager worked with him. His age may have been against him—he emigrated at forty-seven—and his unworldly Old Worldliness. Whatever the hopes and fears that forced him to leave Europe, he died an impoverished and disappointed man, one of the many invisible immigrants unable to adapt in the increasingly prosperous New World. As a boy Houdini was a permanent witness to his father's limitations, to the ways in which his adopted culture closed him out, to the way his past was always shadowing him.

Houdini, escaping from the traditions his father could neither sustain nor be sustained by, suffering the fate of Old World pieties in the fraught commercialism of the New World, discovered a timely opportunism in himself: a personal religion of performed ingenuity. As a young boy he sold newspapers, shined shoes, and ran errands to ease the family's persistent financial worries. But it was a spectacular defiance that he was clearly drawn to, as though his father was a negative ideal for him, and the most melodramatic way of being absolutely unlike his father would be the only way through for him. The family that tried, like so many other families, to assimilate— "to make or be like . . . to conform . . . to take after . . . to become absorbed or incorporated into the system" (OED)—raised (as they may have intended) a child who would defy nature, confound gravity. He would devote his life to the performance of a violent parody of assimilation. He would be the man who could adapt to anything *and* escape from it.

At nine he first performed as a contortionist and tra-
peze artist. He would reshape himself, balance, and return
to normal. He called himself—and this self-renaming
was crucial to the person he was making himself out to
be—Ehrich, The Prince of the Air (as a crossword puzzle
clue to his life, it is worth noting that this new given
name has "rich" as its second syllable, just as "Houdini"
would have "who" as its first). But the father who had
lost his identity as a learned rabbi and been crushed by
financial pressures haunted his son, though not as a story
to be told. "Such hardships and hunger became our lot,"
Houdini remarked later in his life, and "the less said on
the subject the better." Very little was said—there was
a great deal of verbal concealment, of sleight of hand
and word—but many uncanny things were shown and
performed about the confining of lives. The literally
death-defying performances through which he made his
name were organized around the mysterious disappearance of constraints ("He will mystify you if he can. . . .
Houdini, look at him!" said the billboards). And yet he
would, as we shall see, devote the last years of his life to a
personal crusade to discredit spiritualists. The "Greatest
Magician the World Has Ever Seen" wanted people to
look, and to believe their eyes; and then he wanted to persuade them that seeing must not be believing. When it
came to spurious magic—a curious idea in itself, imply-
ing that there is a real magic that is not a confidence
trick—Houdini was very keen to name names. But calling up the dead by name, as the famous mediums were
wont to do, Houdini treated as something akin to a

heresy. He demanded constraints on what people could do with the dead.

There were to be many misspellings of his assumed last name, despite his attempt to call himself something (perhaps after somebody) once and for all: Houdin, Professor Houdinis, Hondini, Hunyadi. It is, of course, common immigrant experience to have little control over what people do with your name, over what they call you. And in Houdini's case there was the added complication that to begin with there were two of them, called the Brothers Houdini. There were to be two sets of the Brothers Houdini, and the first ones were not brothers. First he joined up with a friend, then with his brother Dash (itself an Americanizing of his Hungarian name, Deszö); finally he became a solo act. The actual provenance of the stage name that became him, so to speak, is uncertain, though it is probably a version (an Italian-sounding Americanization) of the name of the French conjurer and founder of modern magic, Jean-Eugène-Robert Houdin. Ehrich's nickname, Ehrie, became Harry, and Harry Houdini was born.

Houdini was to become fascinated by the history and traditions of magic, collecting and archiving material in an extensive library. It was as though the father's life-long commitment to the Jewish tradition was displaced in the son to a countercultural tradition, the theologically suspect tradition of magic. Houdini, as we shall see, attempted to legitimate himself through both promoting and exposing what were from both a religious and a scientific point of view—the two most culturally privileged perspectives—illegitimate practices. Houdini, appropriately enough, became increasingly interested in what magic should be called; in how things (and people) do and don't fit in, literally and metaphorically; in how they get categorized, and find their place.

Asked in a questionnaire in 1909 what his favorite motto was, Houdini answered, "Do others or they will do you." If this was contemporary morality at its starkest, the business ethic in a slogan, it was also, as Houdini often was, unpreciously poetic. Doing others is also what actors and other performers do (magic, as practiced by Houdini in his spectacular shows, made uncanny theater out of his own peculiar mix of science and religion; he did amazing "experiements," exhibiting extraordinary powers). Doing others implies both exploiting them and being like them, with the covert implication that to imitate is to exploit. Parodying the Christian "Do unto others"—and Houdini was a Jew in the new secular Christian world— Houdini's motto is also the motto of the immigrant: perform other people or they will perform you, prejudge you. For Houdini the whole notion of identity, of whom one prefers to be seen as, was something one escaped into from the past. If you are defined by what you can escape from—your country, your language, your poverty, your name—then you may need forever to seek out situations to release yourself from. To defy, in ever-greater feats of ingenuity and endurance, people's descriptions of you. Like Mr. Toad of *The Wind in the Willows,* Houdini was a man of crazes, one of which, unsurprisingly perhaps, was airplanes. He liked to do and to be the new thing. And he liked taking flight.

The trick that first made Houdini's name—that would settle the question of what he should call himself—was called Metamorphosis. And the transformation that actually occurred onstage was a simple exchange, a reversal of roles. In the 1890s he was appearing with his wife as a touring magician, versatile in his range of tricks but drifting towards becoming above all an "escape artist." One newspaper of the time described him as the "American Self-Liberator . . . World's Handcuff King & Prison Breaker—Nothing on Earth Can Hold Houdini a Prisoner." He was the innocent man who could, to entertain and for fame and fortune, escape from the best the penal system had to offer by way of confinement and surveillance. He could get out of anything. And that there was somebody who could do this in America (and Europe, where he would soon tour) sent a peculiarly paradoxical message to the people who flocked to his shows, not to mention the so-called authorities, whom he was, as we shall see, adept at recruiting for his shows. He was not a criminal (or a god); he outwitted the authorities, and was celebrated for doing so. It was the perfect spectacle for any apparently law-abiding society committed to progress. He was the secular and successful Prometheus, inside the law and beyond; he was a picture of the exorbitant entrepreneur, abolishing the category of the impossible; a man who was to help the police, by instruction and challenge, to improve their handcuffs; a man who would mercilessly expose those spiritualists who claimed that they could release the dead from their silence.

But first, he would change places with a woman. (Later he would become part—if not one of the originators and unwitting popularizers—of the iconography of what we now call sadomasochism.) Now, as he began to become Houdini, his metamorphosis was into a man who made his audience wonder what he could do with his body and how he could get a woman into a box.

For Metamorphosis Houdini was tied in a sack and then locked in a trunk by his wife. The trunk was then padlocked, fastened with thick rope, and wheeled into a cabinet. Once Houdini was in his "box," in the words of a contemporary account:

> Mrs Houdini, standing at the open curtain (in front of the cabinet) makes the following brief announcement. "Now then, I shall clap my hands three times, and at the third and last time I ask you to watch CLOSELY for—the—EFFECT." At this she rapidly closes the curtain and vanishes from sight, yet instantaneously the curtain is reopened—this time by Houdini himself.

Where Houdini was, there Mrs. Houdini would be. Tied up in the dark, awaiting her release, which was not part of the show. It was the magic of *his* release that got the applause; his reappearance, not her new predicament, that was, apparently at least, the center of attention (the audience might have been unwittingly applauding what he had done to his wife). "Your attention towards this end of the hall," Harry Houdini would shout in the dime museums and circuses they worked in. "Here you will find a clever young man. . . ."

A woman in a box for a man in a box. To us it seems

almost tritely emblematic in its turning of the tables, in its drama of human bonds as bondage (it would have been a different act with an "assistant" who was known not to be his wife). A man does to a woman what a woman has done to a man: confine him inside something. The act itself has a slight but interesting ambiguity in that his wife uses that curious magic ritual of clapping her hands, as though the *effect* might be in her hands, as it were, rather than in Houdini's extraordinary powers. The man who in 1916 would write and copyright a film treatment entitled *The Marvellous Adventures of Houdini, The Justly Celebrated Elusive American;* the man who wrote to Robert Gould Shaw— whose private library was to form the basis of the Harvard University theater collection—that he wanted to "spread history in an accessible manner, as all roads do not lead to Boston (though all cultured roads do)," was to popular- ize elusiveness as a spectacle. He wanted as many people as possible to watch him being as elusive as possible: to wonder where they would find him next.

Houdini's Metamorphosis—like many of his later and more extraordinary feats—took it for granted that get- ting free was the adventure, not being free. The audience wouldn't pay for long to see Houdini as a free man; indeed, his freedom resided in his (continually) getting free. And he performed being confined by choice. "I have never been arrested," he declaimed on stage in the 1920s. "I have never had anything of any nature against me or mine. I've had to work very hard for everything I have obtained. I come from a race of students and I am not entirely illiterate, and I do read and study." This is poignant in the assurances it wishes to give, but it is also characteristically canny. The ways in which he wants to legitimate himself are conventional; he's not unlettered, he comes from good stock, and he has worked honestly. But such guarantees were only required, such clichés proffered because somewhere Houdini knew that what he was always working on, what he had to work with, was his audience's skepticism. Without scholarship, without any kind of institutional position, uncredentialed, Houdini was in the business of persuasion. But not just any kind of persuasion; he had to conjure states of baffled conviction in the people who paid to watch. They always had to be shown that he could do something, but not how he could do it. He was, in other words, rather like a scientist or a priest, except that he invited scrutiny but never tendered explanations of any sort. He was, as it were, quite patently a mystifier. As he said, he was never arrested, he couldn't be stopped. "I am not a magician," he would say, "but a mystifier." In fact he became notorious for two things that, as we shall see, were connected for him: escaping and boasting ("with due modesty I can say that I recognize no one as my peer"). In the act of boasting he hoped magically to release himself from his lowly, ambiguous status. The boaster, after all, does not wish to be remembered merely for the fact that he boasted.

But Houdini was interestingly selective in his excesses. Though claiming rather too often that he was "not entirely illiterate"—that, presumably, he could read, and like everyone else read some things rather than others—

he turned the perennial philosophical problem of skepticism into a performance art (indeed, street theater, when he would hang chained from a bank in Manhattan). And by making exaggerated claims on people's credulity, by encouraging them to believe the unbelievable, he did something very strange. He showed them that the only cure for skepticism was high risk. "The image by which he remains most often visualized," his biographer Kenneth Silverman writes in *HOUDINI!!!, The Career of Ehrich Weiss,* is that of "a man in white shirt sleeves and dark trousers dangling upside down from a tall building, arms outstretched in a pose of inverted crucifixion." But these high risks created greater uncertainties. People couldn't help but believe what they saw—a respectably dressed man hanging from a skyscraper, those symbols of a certain kind of success, posed as an inverted Christ and getting away with it. And if they believed what they perceived, then Houdini himself, his powers or his skills, were radically unintelligible. They saw, but didn't know what to believe about what they saw.

If you believed in what Houdini could do, what exactly were you believing in? What is a fascination with risk a fascination about? "The easiest way to attract a crowd," Houdini wrote, "is to let it be known that at a given time and a given place someone is going to attempt something that in the event of failure will mean sudden death." To be a good performer one has to know something, in one way or another, about audiences. Houdini always seems to have been intuitively an audience to himself, before he let other people see him. To attract a crowd, and to be attractive to a crowd, as he implies, death has to be on the menu. But it is risk they come to see, it is the drama of failure and success wrought to an unusual pitch. The bullfighter takes on the bull and the limits of his own body; Houdini took on all these significant (symbolic) cultural artifacts—ropes, chains, handcuffs, gags; the holding and containing and punishing devices of the culture—and the limits of his own body. And unlike the bullfighter, he had largely to invent as he went along the skills he needed. He pitted himself against man-made things and his own nature, as a self-made man.

To maintain an audience for what he called his "self-created hazardous work," he knew that he would have to raise the stakes. Metamorphosis would itself go through various metamorphoses, including in 1918 making Jenny the elephant disappear from a cabinet (not merely, Houdini said, "the talk of the town," but "the talk of the show world"). "A creature weighing over 4000 pounds vanishes in full glare of the light," he wrote to a friend, adding with his usual combativeness, "So I am still in the ring." Playing with paralysis as failure—whether as death or as inescapable confinement—and mobility as success, Houdini turned getting away with things into his own art form. He was, that is to say, a thoroughly modern man. "Had I been born of different parentage," he told a reporter, "I might have developed into a very dangerous criminal." Of course, temperamentally, Houdini couldn't imagine himself turning into an ordinary criminal. He wanted to be a respectable outlaw in the country that made that word famous. And to do this, to keep getting out of his boxes, he had to be quick and, as we shall see, he had to be familiar with the law, but not study it as his father had done. He had to be able to get away with things that people couldn't believe.

HE DESCRIBES WHAT is a familiar scenario, at least to him. In his view it represents just what he is like. He is the man who wants to desire as quickly as possible, to get it over with.

He is an academic, and he is giving a lecture. As always, while he is reading his paper he is also scanning the audience for what he calls "the appealing faces." He spots a woman who "interests" him, and then, for the rest of his lecture, refuses to look at her. He remembers, by way of an association, the Peter Cook and Dudley Moore sketch where they are on a bus and Cook says, "That girl over there really fancies me." Moore says, "How do you know?" "Well, she hasn't looked at me once," Cook replies.

After his talk—and this or something like this often

happens—he walks into an adjoining room for a cup of tea, and there she is at the end of the line. It is an ideal opportunity, he barely has to do anything. "As though she was there waiting for me." She smiles, he looks at his watch and affects to have just realized that he is late for something, and flees.

"It may be the transition between desiring a woman in your mind and meeting her in reality that feels bewildering," I say at one point. "It's like preparing to go and see your girlfriend with an afternoon of porn."

He thinks about this. Then he says, "The phrase 'the ecstasy of solitude' has come into my mind. Is that a quote?"

"Quoting is also using other people's lines, getting away from yours."

"Yes, they can be a kind of cover story I suppose," he agrees, slightly grudgingly. "Is it a quote, though?"

As he is leaving he repeats what we discovered several weeks ago was a remark we both loved, made by the British soccer manager Tommy Docherty after a match that his team had won. "They were lucky to get nil."

The basic plot—the plot that stirs him and flusters him and ultimately frustrates him—is his finding someone as soon as possible whom he desires; his coming across her by accident, without his apparently instigating anything, and then his rushing off, usually home. Once he is home, and "free" as he calls it, he feels dreary and enraged. And he cheers himself up by remembering that there are bound to be other occasions in the future when it will be different. And "different" means for him no temptations of failure and no guarantees of success. He will simply allow himself to find out whether he wants or likes the woman, and what it is he is after. He is well aware, that is to say, that "the person whom one desires" can be translated as "the person from whom one wants a great deal (in both senses)." He knows that he is suffering from what he wants, from the uncomfortable pressure of it, and from not knowing what he wants. When he is unwittingly thrown into a position in which he might find out, or even say something, he is distracted by panic. From a commonsense point of view—or rather, from a certain kind of logical point of view—it is obviously puzzling, to put it mildly, that one can so eagerly not want something that one wants. It has become the new "enlightened" common sense that our most urgent project is to escape from our desires. And this is perhaps unsurprising wisdom in consumer societies that above all need people to want. If we must desire, let us desire quickly and briefly. If escaping is what we do, then we can at least become escape artists. We can turn our desire for other people into a desire to elude them. We can decorate our burrows.

As an academic, of course, he is a "great reader," as he ironically puts it. But this was not always the case. He was, he believes, "converted" to reading by explicit pressure from his parents and by two events in his life. One was the "event," as he called it, of his parents' troubled marriage. As for many children, reading soon became something of a refuge for him. But it was clinched as a passion by his discovery, in early adolescence, of a book on his parents' night table called *In Praise of Older Women,* about a series of erotic encounters between a young man and various older women. He couldn't stop reading it and masturbating over it; it was a "revelation." With this book in his bedroom he felt, he said, like one of those seventeenth-century religionists, "in their prayer closets, in a fervor." I said that I thought that they were wanting to be closer to God, and he said, "Yes, exactly," getting my point or missing it. It had been through books he had been able to remember the "ecstasies of the flesh"; in withdrawal he had rediscovered an apparently new, abandoned self (in both senses, which often go together). His relationship to reading seemed more productively interesting—to both of us—than his apparent relationship to either of his parents. Or talking about reading had become the most viable way for him to talk about his affinities to and doubts about himself and other people. He is, needless to say, a very fast reader.

There are, he told me, books one wants to read, books one wants to have read, and books one would like to be the kind of person who could read. He had, he realized once he started talking, given the subject a lot of thought. Books were the kind of object of desire that made him eloquent; they made him curious, and curious about his curiosity about them. They were like stopgaps, he said. There was a mood, he said, that he had been familiar with as long as he could remember (and it was a state of mind in which memory had been abolished, in which memory was not available to revise). He described it as a state of "ravenous boredom" in which he might eat, or phone a friend, or masturbate, knowing all the time that nothing would suffice. In this mood he was prone to browse in bookshops, books being the thing that were most likely to satisfy, to take him out of this "bland, boring melodrama of discontent." I told him that I thought that he wasn't exactly seeking satisfaction, but rather trying to get rid of this discomforting feeling. In what he referred to as his "supermarket mood" he was more like a man on the run—"with the runs," he corrected me, "desperate for a good shit"—someone internally harassed, in which the quest, such as it was, was for relief.

What one is escaping from is inextricable from, if not defined by, what one is escaping to. It seemed that he wanted to persuade me that one can only know what one is escaping from once one has escaped (in fact, once he had escaped, once he had found the book that transformed him, he was "fine," and forgot about the whole thing). I wanted to persuade him to be interested in the problem, not fascinated by the solution; that what he called his "escape claws" was a blind. The self-cure he had found for this restlessness was more like a drink to an alcoholic. But as he pointed out to me, quite rightly, reading had got him (and me) a long way. After all, what was he supposed to do in this mood, just sit in his room, keep still, and hope something better than a book turns up? "Yes," I said, "you might see what else occurs to you."

His mother had been ill as a child, and had become an absorbed reader. He had spent a lot of time at home, one way or another, watching his mother reading. He had inferred that books were what his mother most liked to look at. Books were what she wanted, and therefore presumably liked. He couldn't be a book, alas, but he could get lots of books inside him. Not that his mother ever wanted to talk about books, except in the perfunctory way—which his father mocked, and clearly felt troubled by—of "really liking" some more than others. Her son couldn't be a book, but he could have books. So in the supermarket mood it wasn't clear who or what he was getting a book for, though books were clearly deemed to be the solution to something. I wondered whether his mother might have transmitted to him a conscious interest in books and an unconscious state of mind or range of feeling that books were meant to cure. This seemed plausible to him because sometimes the mood felt like an "imposition." "Like emotional homework?" I asked. "No, like some pointless kind of research. But I managed to turn it to account. I got a lot from these books . . . I made a life out of reading, my mother only made a half-life."

Reading books was like a devotional exercise—they called up a reading self in him that he liked and admired—at once connecting him to his mother and defining him as unlike his father, whom he described with some derisory glee as a "desultory reader, an airport-book man" (even in this, books are linked to transports). But he read books very quickly, "getting in and out as fast as possible," as though lingering was tricky for him. He wasn't sure whether he wanted to read the book or to have read it (to have experiences without having to go through them, or be through with them). And this question had intermittently troubled him, because it was like living in and for the future, when he would have read all the requisite books, when he would be finally equipped. But for what? Books, in other words, were an enigmatic invitation. They made more of a muddled appeal to him than he realized. Reading, whatever else it was, was a sacrificial pleasure.

When he was an adolescent he had found a picture in a pornographic magazine that had stayed with him ("I only have to think of this and I can come anywhere, anytime, with anyone"). It was, he thought, an image of "enticement," but not cruel, because the woman "didn't look as if she was doing anyone a favor . . . even herself." A naked woman is kneeling on a bed on all fours, looking back over her shoulder at the camera. She is smiling, and "her cunt is glistening."

"Glistening?" I asked with that practiced analytic quizzicalness.

"Yes," he said, "as in dew . . . the 'glistening bank.' " (G was his last initial.) "She looks like she's really into something . . . not wanting anything in particular, or obvious . . . She's not attending to anyone, to any-thing . . . so you can forget all the sordidness, all the sleazy people involved in getting the picture . . . You don't have to think that she's some single mum somewhere, earning some pathetic money."

"So it seems to be a picture of someone who's aroused but untroubled . . . as though she's escaped from her own demandingness and other people's. But in another part of your mind there are all the sleazy people. The picture works because it lets you forget those people."

"Yes," he said, "and when I want to actually come I think of them . . . coming gets me out of a nasty corner."

"So coming is coming away from the woman. Thinking of the sleazy people helps you out."

Whatever else I am to him, I am the listening bank in whom he has invested some of his money, and from whom he wants advice about his emotional investments (on one of the rare occasions he said something that he thought was odd, he described himself as "cashing in his dick with a woman"). But he is also the woman in the picture, who appears to be in a state of desire in which, because there is no demand, there is nothing to flee from. Her apparent self-absorption paradoxically frees his desire. He can get happily excited, he believes, because she is not trying to be exciting. As long as nothing smacks of seduction there's nothing to flee. Once the sleazy people turn up—and he knows that without them there would be no picture, that they have done him a kind of favor—then there is something to get away from. And, at least logically, if there were no sleazy people he wouldn't have to come, his desiring would be an end in itself. The sleazy people, whom he imagines (probably rightly) to be all men, seem to be the ones, he thinks, who at least in his fantasy, turn him into what he calls "a conventional heterosexual . . . the man who comes and goes." They want his semen in exchange for his money; they are, he thinks, "buying the masturbator inside him, the man who prefers everything on his own, when there is no one else to spoil it."

"It's odd, isn't it," I say, "the sense we can have that other people are the ones who spoil the things we can't actually do without them."

"If other people weren't there there'd be nothing to

do," he says, "but when they are there you don't know what to do with them."

WHEN FREUD WROTE in his *Three Essays on Sexuality* that the object was "soldered" on to the instinct, he was saying, in his technical way, that the people we desire, the people we are drawn to, are secondary, an afterthought; that we are simply the bearers of free-floating desire that is always seeking its targets; that if we are having a primary relationship with anything, it may not be with other people but with our own desire. Other people are what we attach our wanting to. Freud, in other words, is not saying we don't need other people to do the things we need to do; he is just contesting the sense in which "relationship" is the right word for what we are doing.

Psychoanalysis, of course, does not reveal what people are really like, because we are not really like anything; psychotherapeutic treatment is productive of selves, not only disclosing of selves that have been there all the time waiting to be discovered, like Troy (or Atlantis). The self Freud was listening for, and therefore intrigued by, was the self that was radically puzzled by her links to other people, and to herself (his "method" of free association makes a startlingly simple claim: everything that you thought was important about yourself isn't, and everything you consider to be unimportant is crucial). Either, Freud implies, we take relationships for granted (as some kind of norm), and then try and work out what makes them so difficult and why they go wrong; or we begin to wonder what we are doing with other people and ourselves, and what we want to do with them. If "relation-ship" is not the right word for what we are up to with each other, then we may not be the escape artists we thought we were.

The variously constructed differences between the sexes are often construed in terms of what each sex is deemed to be in flight from in the other (men in flight from acknowledged involvement, women in flight from their ruthlessness, say). And in the emotional geography of (modern) sexual escapism, it is often assumed that people would be better off not running away, that except in the extreme cases of brutality and bullying, there are things that are better confronted (dependency, say, or the inevitability of betrayal and disappointment). The sheer scale of fear between people—the terrors and uncertain-ties people can generate in each other—make a life of exits and more occasional entrances a virtual necessity. Imaginative life is almost exclusively about elsewhere. A person who is running away from something, the psychoanalyst Michael Balint once remarked, is also run-ning towards something else. If we privilege (as psycho-analysts and others do) what we are escaping from as realer—or in one way or another more valuable—than what we are escaping to, we are preferring what we fear to what we seem to desire. Fear of something (or some-one) and the wish to escape from it confer a spectacu-lar reality on it (if you want to escape from someone, they have become very important to you). Things are not frightening because they are real, they are real because they are frightening. Fear always confers power on its object.

Much of our so-called erotic fantasy life appears to be a rather elaborate mapping of our escape routes from sex. Indeed, the fascination of pornography—the most disparaged (and relished) of the popular arts—is that it is the genre in which life rarely imitates art. And yet to talk about escape in this context—or the other evasions and avoidances and elusions—may be too knowing (one can't say that sex with other people is better than masturbation, only that it is better for certain things). If we say that sexual fantasies are or can be used as an avoidance of reality, we must believe we have some privileged sense of what real sexuality involves. As though we might simply deduce what is real by giving an accurate account of what we believe we need to get away from. The whole notion of escapism depends upon there being a reliable account somewhere of what it is necessary for us to face up to (and then we need a further account of what that facing up to can do for us: what kind of better life it has in store for us). The bracing language of engagement and confrontation and courage requires, if it is to be used without irony, a strong sense of just what it is we are supposed to be up against, and an impressive account of what's so important about it.

The photograph that had captured this man's imagination, that crystallized (or formulated) his personal mysticism about sexuality, was, as such things always are, a kind of memory. It was an image at once over-wished, and so representing an ideal for himself, and documentary, in that it encoded something of his history (we are only captured by what we have once been or wanted to be). Indeed, he once said to me that it must sound as though "there are no real women in my story." And then he added, without wistfulness, without an escape hatch of irony, "But it's not against the law to invent people."

MYTHS ARE OFTEN ABOUT the inescapable, about the painful discovery of powerful constraints. They tend not to be stories about people who get away with things, but rather stories about people who try to; people whose transgressions turn out to be a lesson for us all. Oedipus, Prometheus, Narcissus, and Antigone, all in their different ways, suffer the most violent of sentimental educations. That there must be some things that no creature can elude—whether they be laws (natural or moral), desires (variously deemed moral or immoral), or biological limits (the need to breathe, eat, and die)—and that they must be discovered, recognized, and observed are integral to our sense of ourselves and the ways in which we question who we are. When a constraint can be described as something else—when the earth becomes round so we can't fall off it, when the notion of sin is seen to be a devious form of social control, and so on—we change our place in the world. When a constraint can't be redescribed, it can make the world, the way things are despite our intentions, seem more robust, more solid. (What we want to know about a transgression is, what's the difference, what remains the same after the act?) It was part of Houdini's allure to offer popular spectacles of the safe but shocking transgression. He could amaze people but leave everything as it was. He could break the rules of possibility, break out of the best jails in the land, and earn the admiration of the police.

Houdini enacted and reenacted—but with a twist— something that is essential to many of the myths of his father's tradition (the stories of Abraham, Moses, and Jonah, not to mention the classical myths of Oedipus and Icarus): a flight from something that will be returned to. In these formative stories that are stories of everyday life, the initial wish to escape is a form of recognition. As in any erotic encounter, it is because something (or someone) has been so powerfully acknowledged, so starkly registered, that it must be fled from. The impulse to get away is both a furtive intelligence and a precondition for return. Resisting someone, even if it is God or the gods, refusing someone in the first instance, is the only way of thinking about them. The wish to run away is a sign of affinity. The wish to return—the escape artist Houdini's motive—in one way or another seals the hero's, the heroine's, the prophet's fate. But what Houdini kept returning to, in a kind of parody of the hero myth, was another and yet more demanding escape. As the Don Juan of his own devices, his acts were an unspoken commentary on the whole notion of progress, which, along with liberty, was the much-touted ideal of his and his father's adopted country. Houdini's revelation was always himself, and he had to keep producing it. Was the escape artist a more-of-the-same artist, like Sisyphus, or was he an innovator? Or had escape become an end in itself, and escape acts like his own—though there were none like his, he would always insist—the ultimate, indeed the exemplary commodity? You could now pay to watch a man escape so as to escape again; a man who was liberating himself only to be able to liberate himself again later. His ideal, his project, was survival, in order to go on earning his living by performing ever more difficult feats. He would not be dropped by America, he would drop himself off its highest buildings, the symbols of its success.

"Eventually," Houdini remarked, "one sinks slowly into the habits of the country in which one lives and I know my work suffers." Houdini feared the assimilation that was slowness, and dreaded getting stuck. As immigrants, his family struggled to learn the habits without drowning, without something else in them—called by Houdini "the work"—being drowned out. The work was essentially the devising of ever more unusual, exacting, and marketable "tricks" that would, in an unwitting way, exploit and expose the habits of the country. There were, for example, the penal system, psychiatric institutions, and the frozen food business, all of which, in

apparently unrelated ways, required methods of confinement. From outside their institutions, from outside any
institution, Houdini would use their various artifacts—
handcuffs, straitjackets, ice—to devise what he called
"some new unthinkable escape" in which "the audience
never knows whether the stunt is hard or easy." Making the "unthinkable" a necessity, if not a virtue, Houdini might make his audience wonder what it was that
made something unthinkable; and why now the unthinkable had become so salable. His new country was
amazingly adept at inventing new things to escape from—
unthinkable things, until someone thought of them, and
mystifying if no one could explain them. If the audience must never know whether the stunt was hard or
easy, they never knew whether anyone could do it or only
someone special; whether it was accessible or esoteric,
whether it was only for the chosen or an opportunity for
all. In other words it was left ambiguous whether Houdini was sowing the seeds of anarchy—the streets seeth-
ing with escaped criminals and lunatics—or reassuring
the forces of law and order. It was part of his enigmatic
message to the audience, though, that if you want to be
skillful at escaping you have to get yourself confined first.
After all—as Houdini's stunts both advertise and make
one forget—why do people normally want to escape?
And, perhaps more to the point (though more concealed
by the stunt), what do they, these people, do once they
have escaped?

One of the ways Houdini both reassured his audience
and mystified them at the same time was by devising

stunts in which he didn't destroy the thing he was escaping from. Everything would look the same, except
that he would now be outside rather than inside the
confinement. He would break out but nothing would be
broken. So in the early trick Metamorphosis, there would
be no mess on stage, no evidence; it would be the perfect
(non)crime. So the audience would be quite unable, from
what they could actually witness, to reconstruct just
what he had done and how he had done it. All they could
see was the result of a hidden process; the struggle, the
ingenuity, the trickery of the man in the box were all
hidden.

In 1912, his biographer Kenneth Silverman tells us,

> he sought German patents for a watertight chest on
> four legs, which would be locked and then lowered into
> a larger chest, which would be locked, and filled with
> water too. The performer would thus be islanded, dry,
> inside the smaller chest, but surrounded on all sides by
> the water in the outer box. Houdini's design allowed
> him to escape from both boxes without damaging the
> locks—and without becoming wet. He also applied for
> a patent on a kind of theatrical deepfreeze . . . a device
> by which he could be frozen inside a block of ice yet
> walk away leaving the block whole—a miracle he
> would try to work out his entire life.

If he wasn't busy being born in these boxes he was busy
dying. Neither of these tricks was ever actually performed, and in a sense this makes them even more interesting. They are the impossible dreams of the greatest

escapologist, the miracles, the fantasies that he was unable to translate into reality, patented so that no one else would have the chance. Houdini's fear of being imitated, to which we will return—his need to be unique, unprecedented, unthinkable—was matched by his desire not to imitate himself too much. He was a tireless inventor of things that might defeat him, of traps that could kill him. And all these stunts, as he called them—the word itself meaning a performance, a feat, an event, but also "a check in growth . . . a state of arrested development" (OED)—had that kind of uncanny symbolic resonance that made him an irresistible spectacle, a unique draw in a newly emerging and ever more powerful entertainment industry (Houdini would eventually start his own Film Development Corporation). He was determinedly and calculatingly a spirit of the age, but by using a vocabulary of familiar cultural objects—chests, trunks, beds, locks, ice (for freezing and preserving food)—he seemed to speak the strange language they seemed to encode, as though the drama of the age was claustrophobia, of the confinement created by new kinds of freedom. The magic was to escape without damaging the locks, without even chipping the ice. It could all be done without violence, everything would seem the same. The grand illusion was that nothing had changed—neither Houdini nor his box—but everything was different. It was literally a revolution—a radical and irreversible reordering, and a repetition of the same thing unmodified, without apparent struggle. It was magic, an art form in which success was the concealment of difficulty, and the difficulty was deception.

It is perhaps not surprising, given the peculiar combination of his temperament and his family history, that Houdini should have been so fascinated by the essentially theatrical systems of social control that his country prided itself on. When Houdini entered his contraption and after he had escaped, the audience would see no signs of panic, rage, or terror on his face. His composure, his genial self-control, were part of the rigor of his art. By the same token, as it were, he was drawn, like many assimilated Jews of his generation—which was also the generation of the early psychoanalysts—to those people who had lost the ability or the willingness to conform: the mad and the criminal. In some of his stunts he would pretend to be such a person, engaged in improvising an escape. But when he was aping the mad, the struggle was there for everyone to see; this, clearly, Houdini wanted to expose as an ordeal.

He devised, often attended by real hospital orderlies and asylum attendants, "an escape from a so-called crazy-crib, a strong, light bedstead used in hospitals and insane asylums to restrain exceptionally violent patients." He was strapped to a mattress with leather around his middle, ankles, and thighs; his arms were crossed over his chest and then belted, his wrists strapped to the frame. His neck was strapped down with a leather collar to the bed. After wriggling for twenty-five minutes, as a London newspaper reported it,

> his hands blue, his face livid, . . . everybody thought the task impossible. The next moment and the bed slipped from its position, and Houdini, all but choked

to death, had to gasp for the bed to be replaced in its original position. Then started an awesome struggle for supremacy. At twenty five minutes, by almost a super-human effort, he got the neck collar adrift, and writh-ing like a snake, opened the buckles of his wristlets with his teeth, and in five minutes later he was entirely free, very nearly exhausted, and with his evening clothes, from his shirt to his trousers, literally torn in ribbons he walked down the stage.

His evening clothes ruined, his respectability in tat-ters, Houdini was to all appearances as sane afterwards as he was before, though he had been engaged in some-thing quite insane for over half an hour. His contortion and his plain suffering—"his hands blue, his face livid . . . writhing"—seem now like a curiously tasteless initiation rite, or even a human sacrifice. If he showed how be-ing confined like this might give someone a violently mad desire to escape, it also consoled the audience that only a sane person like Houdini could actually wriggle free. The violently mad person, ideally, would be the person unable to escape from such a "crib." The audience recruited by Houdini—and perhaps vice versa—was doing a bit of consumer research into its mental health provisions.

In another mental health stunt, the "most releastic [sic] challenge I ever presented"—after which he became known as the Great Escape Artist—he got the hospital attendants to roll him in sheets with only his head uncov-ered and then tie him to the metal frame of a hospital bed. The orderlies would then pour about twenty buckets of hot water over him, dousing the sheets so they would shrink and tighten. This was all done outside his cabinet, the box that conventionally both hid and contained his efforts, so the audience could see what his biographer describes as the "muscle-wrenching turning and squirming to loosen the skintight sheets." It was like watching a man trying to wriggle out of his own skin. "Dangerous to health," Houdini noted of this trick.

The hospital bed stunt was indeed a challenge, but it is curious that Houdini should have considered it his most realistic. What was the real thing, the real experience that was being demonstrated, or even alluded to? What was wrapping someone in sheets, tying them to the kind of bed in which they were supposed to be looked after, and pouring buckets of water over them, realistic of? Reading this scenario, one might associate the sheets with winding sheets, being tied to a hospital bed with what happens to the criminally insane, and pouring buckets of water over something with putting out a fire. It was like a (just pre-Dada) Dadaist drama about the emergency services. But it was also a scene in which a man chooses to torture himself so as to entertain other people, and make a living. The audience watched a man writhing—it was a safe risk, there were people in attendance, real hospital workers there, and a performer who was acting and not acting—but it was manifestly a physically punishing ordeal that people paid to see. Houdini wouldn't die attempting this stunt, but he might suffer and still be defeated by the "challenge." At worst the audience would lose their belief in him, their puzzled and puzzling regard for what he, and only he, would even attempt, let alone do. What was at stake here, amid all the canny and uncanny symbolism of the act that pretended to no greater significance than its own success, was failure. He might hurt himself, and suffer a humiliating setback to the momentum of his career, a career based on never being stuck, always knowing the next move. "I have tried through many a sleepless night," Houdini wrote, telling us about that other ordinary torture on a bed, "to invent schemes to make an audience appreciate some worthy effort of mine." It was essential to Houdini's complicated ambition to be worthy, and to make the effort.

Houdini was tapping into a market for torture. Of course, people wouldn't pay to see the spectacle of one person torturing another—though the attendants always present at his stunts were, theatrically speaking, ambiguously silent witnesses and accomplices of his ordeals—but they were more than happy to watch someone torturing himself. That self-inflicted pain should be more acceptable, more entertaining, more of a commodity, was another thing that Houdini was, in his peculiar way, drawing to people's attention without his or their appearing to notice. It's obviously not suffering we find distasteful or morally objectionable, but imposing it on others. Houdini offering his self-torture to an audience—an act at once discreetly religious and overtly punitive, in the absence of any known crime—was not considered to be in any way an offensive imposition.

What many people considered to be his greatest escape act he called, with undisguised reference, the Chinese

Water Torture Cell. He was always "curious," his biographer says calmly, about mutilation, deformity, and the more vivid forms of brutality:

> He collected articles about an armless artist who could paint with his teeth, a Cannon Ball King whose cannon misfired, crushing his legs. He pasted in his diary a grisly photo of pirates decapitated by Chinese officials, the cutoff heads strewn on the ground like cabbages. In an envelope labelled "Chinese Tortures" he kept a set of revolting snuff snapshots that showed chunks of flesh being hacked from a woman tied to a stake. . . .

His hidden store of images was of people who couldn't escape. And even if there is a sense in which in his mind he was both tormented and tormentor, it was pictures of the victims that he collected and kept. These were the nightmare scenarios that he enacted and mastered each night in his show. After one of these shows (in 1908) the wildly enthusiastic audience wanted a speech. "When there is no more left of Houdini," he said simply, "you may think of me as having done something to entertain you." Like a court fool telling a courteous riddle, he told the audience about their own secret violence; he told them that what they wanted, what gave them such wild pleasure, was flirting with his own death. He had given everything for their amusement, for their innocent sadistic pleasure.

The Water Torture Cell was a body-sized cabinet, full of water, "in appearance much like a small glass phonebooth." He was locked inside, hanging by his ankles, upside down (he also called the trick "the Upside Down" and patented it as a one-act play in England entitled *Houdini Upside Down*). In what he referred to as his "Emperor of Sympathy-Enlisters" voice, he would introduce the theatrically elaborate act—which required 250 gallons of water, an ax, and three assistants—by saying:

> Ladies and Gentlemen in introducing my original invention the Water Torture Cell, although there is nothing supernatural about it, I am willing to forfeit the sum of one thousand dollars to anyone who can prove that it is possible to obtain air inside of the Torture Cell when I am locked up in it in the regulation manner after it has been filled with water.

There was, as often with Houdini, a disclaimer about supernatural powers, a challenge to the audience's skepticism offered, as it were, in the currency that got them into the show, and an unironic allusion to some legitimating authority (what exactly is the "regulation manner" for locking people up in cabinets full of water?). He would then make it clear that his assistants knew how long he could hold his breath for:

> One of them watches through the curtains ready in case of emergency with an axe, to rush in, demolishing the glass, allowing the water to flow out in order to save my life. I positively and honestly do not expect any accident to happen, but we all know accidents will happen and when least expected.

All these realistic reassurances proffered by Houdini created, as it were, the illusion of realism, as though he were saying, this is neither a religious (supernatural) nor a theatrical event, in fact it is more akin to a scientific experiment (Houdini would invite a large "committee" onstage, as part of the stunt, to investigate the apparatus). But it would be that absurd thing, a successful scientific experiment with no available explanation. And the experiment would begin with the orchestra playing "Asleep in the Deep." It was a mixed-media, mixed-genre event. Within two minutes and thirty seconds, Houdini would burst from the cabinet, drenched in water, undrowned. It seemed simply incomprehensible. A German reviewer called it "uncommonly astonishing and awe-inspiring . . . a trick of incredible cunning." Houdini, who was serious about what he did and would often think of himself as at once a magician and a kind of hero-scholar, thought it was his ultimate invention. "I believe it is the climax of all my studies and labours," he wrote. "Never will I be able to construct anything that will be more dangerous or difficult for me to do." Deprived of room, mobility, and air, he had to stay competent while holding his breath. It was in every sense an excessive challenge: too much water, no air, and very little time. The terror of impending suffocation, of drowning in public, had been made thrilling. The torture referred to in the title of the stunt, given the presence of the ax and the assistants, was also the torture of failure, of losing his place in the public eye. What his audience always came to see him escape from was shame, of not being up to his difficult and dangerous inventions. Perhaps this is the meaning of the curious inappropriateness—not to mention gratuitous racism—of his title for the trick. Chinese water torture is very, very slow, and Houdini's escape was defined by its speed. But failure can be a kind of slow torture, and shame is long.

There were then two kinds of stunts for Houdini: the stunt without visible suffering, in which the struggle was invisible, Houdini emerging innocent and unscathed; and the stunt, like the crazy-crib, that exhibited torment. In the first, Houdini cast himself as the respecter of property; there was no damage to himself or his props. In the other there was vandalism, and Houdini exposed his ingenious dexterity, and, not incidentally, his superb physique and physical strength.

But there was a third kind of stunt that helped make Houdini's name that was a combination of these two styles, these two sides of himself. It involved the law (in the early years of his career he had published an appropriately ghostwritten book called *The Right Way To Do Wrong*). "I defy," he would say, as an entirely innocent man, "the police departments of the world to hold me. . . . I challenge any police official to handcuff me." In these escapes from jails and handcuffs, what Houdini was implicitly questioning was not whether the police could catch criminals, but whether they could hold on to them. And if they couldn't, what then would be the point of catching them? In a covert parody of law enforcement, the police would be seen by the public restraining an innocent man who could all too easily escape their clutches.

Houdini, the son of an ex-lawyer, defined himself by his virtually parodic relationship to law enforcement.

"If anyone ever deserved to have a name that is myself. I have spent thousands advertising my name, have broken out of fifteen jails," he claimed, constructing as ever a strange profile of himself. He advertised the name he deserved—Houdini is always interesting about the deserving of names—as that of an innocent lawbreaker, someone, legitimated by the police, playing at breaking the law. What Houdini showed, but didn't tell, was that legitimating oneself, making one's name, was itself a curious game. If a criminal escaped from prison he was punished; if Houdini escaped from prison he was fulsomely rewarded. And in celebrating Houdini's skill the audience was applauding a talent that was potentially a threat to society.

By escaping so well, Houdini positively reframed the absconding criminal as a skilled man, if not an actual artist. He would print testimonials from the police as part of his extensive advertising campaigns. He would boast of his personal connections with law officers. "It has been my good fortune," he wrote, "to meet personally and converse with the chiefs of police and the most famous detectives in all the great cities of the world." He would go to the Policemen's Ball in New York, and kept a *Directory of Police and Prisons.* At the same time, he would, of necessity, as it were, be honing his criminal skills, to earn an honest living. He frequently socialized with criminals in New York on their release from jail, to learn what they knew ("I carry a lot of burglar tools in my baggage").

Houdini made "escapes from unusual cuffs" his spe-
ciality; magic was a suspect art form for him, and his
manufactured escapes were the apotheosis of his art. "I
practice [card tricks] seven or eight hours a day," he told a
reporter from the *Denver Times,* "as conscientiously as a
Paderewski at the piano. But my handcuff tricks are best."
And he liked, above all, to include the officials in these
stunts (just as, when he went to an "Insane Ward" in Cali-
fornia to do a straitjacket trick, he asked the superinten-
dent to strap him in). In a mixing of genres, Houdini
asked the chief of a New Brunswick, New Jersey, police
station to lock him in a "maniac cuff and belt" from a
local asylum. But more often he would simply, with the
press and other police in attendance, invite the officers to
use their best cuffs on him and lock him in their highest-
security jail. Then, often minutes later, he would be out.
In many ways, the credibility of the police in these exhibitions was more at risk than Houdini's reputation.

By 1910, with too many people beginning to imitate his
new, overtly criminal art form, Houdini left the field, but
vengefully. "NO HANDCUFFS," he would advertise on
his posters; and he published a 110-page illustrated book
with the ironic title *Handcuff Secrets.* Affecting to hope that
his readers might become "adepts at entertaining and
mystifying their friends"—where, after all, were they
going to get hold of all these cuffs?—he was in fact dis-
qualifying his rivals (not to mention the handcuff mak-
ers, and the police); and by the same token, committing
the cardinal sin among magicians of exposing techniques
(a manual of magic is a contradiction in terms; what it

tells you is that there is no magic). The book was a characteristic performance in that it gave things away, but kept
his secrets. "I shall not delve into the very deep intricacies
of some of the great modern feats of handcuff manipula-
tions and jail-breaking as accomplished by myself." He
was going to open the subject up by keeping the most
important "intricacies" back, at the same time as putting
many magicians out of a job. The rhetoric steers just clear
of the fever forms of magical mystery-speak; it is more
suggestive of technical skill than hocus pocus.

Despite the "honesty" of his book, it got him into
a great deal of trouble with other magicians and with
the law. Under the guise of exposing magic tricks, Houdini was popularizing criminal methods. The German
authorities banned his illustrations of lockpicks, and the
London *Times* reported that a copy of the book had been
found in the home of two thieves. "I can hardly understand," the prosecuting attorney at their trial pointed
out, "how such a book can be published by such well-
known publishers as Messrs. Routledge. It is a book on
technical education in the art of thieving" (the prosecu-
tor inadvertently colluding with Houdini's sense that it
was indeed an art). The court considered publication of
Handcuff Secrets as "a wrong to the community."

In his arch innocence Houdini was to forge the link,
in a most unexpected way, between crime and entertainment. To claim, simply and straightforwardly, to be
entertaining people was to be the new innocence, the
cover story that he would promote and expose at the
same time. His ferocious wish to expose fraudulence and

hypocrisy, the parallel text to his passion for magic, would find its final target towards the end of his life, as we shall see, in his crusade against the new modern pseudoscience and pseudomagic of spiritualism. He needed to expose what people could do with their hands.

If Houdini was a promiscuous double agent, a spy in both camps—within the law but beyond it, a committed magician who wrote deliberately popular books about magic, an authority on fraudulence—he was also, perhaps by the same token, a shrewdly naive artist, astonishingly adept at exploiting (in both senses) the values, the institutions, and the technologies of his culture. He seems, at least in retrospect, to have staged the kitschiest of dreams with the crassest of meanings. Men were indeed everywhere in chains, he was showing us, but they had created their chains, and they could lose them. Their favorite spectacle was suffering and confinement, transformed into entertainment. It was the age of the hidden powers of sex and money, and the age of overexposure. Even the ritual of his stunts seems quintessentially modern: first the public, open inspection to show that nothing is being concealed; then the spectacle, the evidence of the successful act which proves that either nothing was hidden or that whatever was hidden couldn't be seen. And so we wonder what we are looking for when we are looking at; we wonder what constitutes a mystery—what exceptional powers a person might be thought to have—when no supernatural powers are either invoked or credited.

There is no such thing as magic, Houdini was saying,

but I am a magician capable of inexplicable feats; there is nothing concealed, you can see everything, but you still don't know. It is not too much to say that what Houdini did, to the crowds who flocked to see him—and he became one of the most famous persons in America, a "name," as he would say—was a form of hypnotism. And by the same token he was revealing something horrifying about the nature of fascination, about spectacle as vicarious risk, about the appetites of a modern paying audience. Above all, he shows us, the audience wants to know that it can't see, wants to thrill to its ignorance.

And yet Houdini's invention of himself included his own brand of innocence. He was, symbolically or not, in chains, but he wanted to liberate nothing, no one but himself. There was apparently no political agenda, it was in the fullest sense show business. Despite the blatant sexuality of some of his tricks—his much-vaunted attention to his physique, his state of undress, and his dressing up—his performances were not seen as lewd or suggestive. His unique shows offered a peculiar kind of escapism. His audiences could watch an endangered body willingly struggle with its vulnerability, and apparently not be implicated (as though the magic of money was that paying bought you moral exemption). There could be nothing more preposterous to the spectators than the idea that Houdini was performing the profound existential questions of their culture. Out of his father's and forefathers' tradition of interpretation and observance of the law, as it met with an expansive capitalist culture, he was enacting what he would never have called philosophical or existential dilemmas. But it was philosophy as an odd mixture of dream and mime, using, as dream and mime do, the most potent symbolic props in the culture: jails, beds, trunks, skyscrapers (Houdini often hung himself from the cornices of banks and newspaper offices), chains, cuffs, evening suits, straitjackets—the paraphernalia of the confined body.

What was dramatized above all in Houdini's life of continual allegory, of continual advertisement—"the Napoleon of advertising," a German newspaper called him—was a man losing and refinding some room, a man shrinking his space and then recovering his expansiveness, a man compulsively reinventing and reenacting his own confinement. A man who escaped for money.

ONE OF THE MOST striking features of people who suffer from claustrophobia is that for them, the way out is not through the door. Knowing where the exits are can ease the anxiety, but it rarely cures it. Few rooms are actually incarcerating, but for the claustrophobic person it is as though spaces are always experienced—in a sense must be experienced—as confined. One can feel contained by something enclosing, but the claustrophobic person can only feel persecuted. There is something in the room that has to be fled from, but it appears to be in the space itself. Apparently, the only convincing cure for this malady, from the sufferer's point of view, is flight, is to get out. The claustrophobic person is therefore an amateur escape artist. He needs, in order to survive psychically, to be ingenious and inventive about his exits and entrances.

IN 1909, the year before Houdini gave up his handcuffs, his compatriot and contemporary, the Hungarian psychoanalyst Sándor Ferenczi, wrote a technical "scientific" paper for the *Yearbook of Psychoanalysis*. The paper, called "Introjection and Transference," describes a paradoxical process observed by Ferenczi in which people can both extend and narrow the range of their interests in order to escape from acknowledging what most urgently preoccupies them. The world opens for them to better conceal something. Ferenczi writes:

> So as to keep unconscious various affective connections with certain objects that concern him closely, he [the neurotic] lavishes his affects on all possible objects that do not concern him.
>
> In analysing a neurotic one often succeeds in tracing out historically this extension of the circle of interest. Thus I had a patient who was reminded of sexual events of childhood by reading a novel and thereupon produced a phobia of novels, which later extended to books altogether, and finally to everything in print. The flight from a tendency to masturbate caused in one of my obsessional patients a phobia of toilets (where he used to indulge this tendency): later there developed from this a claustrophobia, fear of being alone in any closed space. I have been able to show that psychi-

cal impotence in very many cases is conditioned by
the transference to all women of the respect for the
mother or sister. With a painter the pleasure of gazing
at objects, and with this the choice of his profession,
proved to be a "replacement" for objects that as a child
he might not look at.

Two things are being said here about two ways of concealing an unacceptable desire. What Ferenczi wants to
emphasize is that one avoids something because it is a
reminder. So the phobia has to extend from novels to all
printed words in order to conceal certain sexual events of
childhood. But there is a useful ambiguity in his description of the way someone might "lavish his affects [feel-
ings] on all possible objects that do not concern him."
There is the straightforward negative sense in which print
doesn't concern this person at all, except insofar as it
reminds him of that novel. But there is a positive sense in
which one might actively engage with many things—
painting, in his example—just to get away from the troubling memory. I might have to avoid toilets and develop
claustrophobia to escape a wish to masturbate (but this in
itself might make me peculiarly inventive in finding new
habits). Is the painter replacing his youthful, forbidden
voyeurism by becoming a painter, or is he concealing
it? Has he translated his desires—moved them across
from, say, looking at his father's body to looking at other
things—or has he substituted them? Whichever it is, he
has held on to looking. The claustrophobic person has
held on to her fearing, to that acute form of excitement

that seeks release through flight. If looking for the painter, like fearing for the claustrophobic person, is the main desire, the primary pleasure, then nothing is concealed by their so-called symptom. Indeed, it isn't a symptom. The object of desire is fear itself, and like all states of excitement it seeks release. Perhaps this is one of several things Ferenczi might have meant, knowingly or unknowingly, when he wrote to Freud in 1908, "Your theory about the origins of phobia . . . finds its analogy in the Hungarian proverb, 'It is better to fear than to be frightened.' "

PHOBIAS REMIND US, in all their unreasonable urgency and their frantic commitment to safety, just how fundamental a sense of our avoiding things is to our sense of ourselves. We are all too familiar with ourselves as escape artists. Knowingly or otherwise we map our lives—our gestures, our ambitions, our loves, the minutest movements of our bodies—according to our aversions, our personal repertoire of situations, encounters, or states of mind or body that we would do anything not to have to confront. As though our lives depend, above all, on accurate knowledge of what we are endangered by. In wishfulness, in the elsewheres of the imagination, we are either choosing our dangers or we are out of harm's way. And yet the irony that the irrational phobia exposes is that the hardest thing to escape from is the wish to escape, that the imaginative activity involved in flight can blind us to any knowledge of quite what it is we are escaping from, and of any way of finding out about it. Indeed, that is its function. When it doesn't starkly and literally save our lives—when we shoot our approaching lion—fear sustains our ignorance. Taboos incite and baffle our curiosity; that is their power. It is escapism itself that is hypnotic. What is being escaped from is often, as Ferenczi suggests, shrouded in mystery. It is as though if we can keep ourselves sufficiently busy escaping, we can forget that that is what we are doing. The opposite of fear, one could say, is choice.

Most modern Western theories about so-called human nature organize themselves around what they consider to be subject to choice; and then they give an account of what all those things that aren't subject to choice might be subject to (God, nature, genes, and so on). And clearly, how we describe our sources has consequences for what we do. God seems to be a choice maker in a way that nature isn't; we think of genes as having functions rather than making decisions. If God is omnipotent he has nothing to fear, though he does create fear in the people he has created, and why he should have needed to do this is of some interest. Even if he gave us what was once called free will—the capacity to make genuine choices and to live by our preferences—he made us creatures who could fear him. So we are at once ruled by intimidation and free to invent our versions of freedom. The founding and fading myth of Adam and Eve is a great escape story, the story of a failed breakout. Transgression is the attempt to find out exactly what it is that is impossible to escape from. In seeking forbidden knowledge about God's creation they discovered just what there was to fear about

God. The biblical story dramatizes, whatever else it does, the link in our minds between curiosity and release, and how our ideas of freedom depend upon our finding out what we have to fear. We find out what the world is like by testing it, by testing ourselves against it.

FERENCZI ACKNOWLEDGES THAT the pleasure of escaping can replace, can always be a good enough substitute for, the pleasure one flees. It is part of the imaginative ingenuity of so-called symptoms that they provide a peculiar kind of satisfaction (you can sometimes tell from their telling just how much people can relish their terrors and their frustrations). And yet Ferenczi is doubly optimistic. He believes that there is actually something there—a fantasy, an experience—that he could help his claustrophobic patient discover (or reconstruct) that would explain his fear to him; that is, show him just what made those desires, that relationship feel so dangerous. And that knowing this, in some sense, would bring him a preferable life. The analysis of his fear would lead to the recovery of himself as a responsible and responsive agent of his own life. If he can have the courage of his curiosity, he will no longer be driven. Knowledge as the cure for our potentially demonic nature: choice as health.

Two questions implicitly preoccupy Ferenczi. First, what is there to escape from in modern lives? (And by implication, how do people go about doing it?) And his psychoanalytic answer to this is that the people he saw were in flight from the sexual desire evoked by family life. And to do this people had to come up with a repertoire of avoidance strategies called defenses, and a repertoire of artifacts called symptoms. But the second question is more difficult to answer: What, if any, are the alternatives to flight, to becoming that characteristically modern escape artist called a neurotic? And if there are no alternatives—and there certainly don't seem to be any from a psychoanalytic point of view—then what is it that makes the successful escape artist, or what are to be our criteria for success?

Acculturation, after all, seems to be about learning what to avoid. Swallowing and spitting out, digesting and evacuating, accepting and rejecting, moral and aesthetic discrimination—this seems to be a natural (developmental) sequence. It is impossible to imagine a person, or indeed a society, that does not have a category of the unacceptable, that does not spend much time producing elaborate descriptions of what is not wanted and how to exclude it. Child rearing is about warding off danger when possible; education teaches how to keep the right distance from certain kinds of beliefs, desires, thoughts, and even people. And to learn to discriminate, to learn to talk and think and choose, is to learn to exclude (attention is supremely selective). So how does something (or someone) become unacceptable, and what else can we do with the unacceptable but rid ourselves of it, get away from it, or get it away from us?

These modern escape artists, the neurotics—and their more fervent risk takers, the so-called perverts—are suffering, are abiding by an absurd and sometimes tragic logic. They are driven by a daunting misapprehension. They don't realize that we don't always flee from something because it is unacceptable; sometimes it is unacceptable to us *because we flee from it.*

THERE ARE PEOPLE who can be defined by what they escape from, and people who are defined by the fact that they are forever escaping. And people tend to describe their compulsory (and compulsive) avoidances—their range of hazards—in terms of personal failure, as though strength of character were straightforwardly equated with the direction in which we run. Our best selves approach; the timid, the lazy, the deceitful retreat. In the geography of our moral lives we need good directions. Our moral vocabularies describe bodies moving in space, learning what to avoid, and, if need be, dispense with. Our first fears turn into habits of evasion, and out of these habits an identity is cast. But this sense of ourselves that we suffer, the private pleasures of who one happens to be, depends for its surety on a double forgetting.

We have to forget what it is we are escaping from—which kinds of feeling, of mood and memory, of desire and encounter—and, ideally, we need to forget that escaping is what we are doing. Our preferences have to be a good cover story for our terrors. Addicts—of work and money, of drink and drugs, of political ideology and fundamentalist religion—are the heroes and antiheroes, the spirits of the age. They (we) enact and dramatize our dilemmas about freedom and memory, about what kind

of freedom is possible, and about how this is bound up
with what any given society (any education) persuades us
is worth getting away from, or, indeed, worth abolishing
so that it is no longer there, apparently, to affront us. If we
happen to live in a society that prefers artists to drug deal-
ers, then either we won't think of art as escapist or we will
have more or less tacitly agreed that whatever the art in
question has released us from is unacceptable, that the
lives we want depend upon avoiding, say, poverty, ugli-
ness, guilt, complexity, or frivolousness. A tradition is a
way of remembering—through taboos and permissions
and encouragements and sacrifices—what it is about ourselves that we are supposed to value and to cultivate. But
it is often the power of such messages that makes us forget that there is always a messenger, and that people who
send messages never quite know what they mean.

WHEN THIS MAN CAME to see me he told me he had been sent by his girlfriend. Or rather, by his ex-girlfriend. He wondered whether this was revenge or social work on her part—whether she wanted him to find out exactly what he was really like so he could see the havoc of his ways, so he could be inflicted on himself for once, or whether she wanted him and "his next ex," as she called her, to get a better deal. He came, he told me, from a tradition of clueless marryers, of people who were "no good at relationships." But, he added, he didn't think relationships were things to be good at.

I asked him what he had found relationships were good for.

He paused and then said with some deliberation, "Grief, sex, and confusion."

63

He told me he had had a dream the previous night in which he was flying from Paris on the Concorde, and the captain announced that on this flight they had finally broken the record for the slowest-ever Channel crossing, and everyone clapped, even the stewardesses. He found himself wondering in the dream if the captain had taken his hands off the steering wheel in order to clap. And then he woke up.

I asked what Paris made him think of.

"Nothing much. Croissants, french letters . . . I used to go to Paris for grubby weekends . . . intellectuals with enviable sex lives . . . That's about it."

I asked him if he had thought about having children, because in the dream he seemed to be in flight from french letters.

"I'm from that tribe they found who don't see any connection between sex and having children."

I asked if he had any children.

He replied, his voice baffled by a kind of dread, that he feared he might have a child, but he had always made himself "untraceable . . . or at least I persuaded the women that they wouldn't want me as a father."

I said I thought there might be a sense that he might be looking after the women and the children by disappearing, that his vanishing acts were a kind of damage limitation.

Having now lost his jauntiness, he seemed momentarily interested in this. "I once had this daydream of all my past women getting together and forming a sort of utopia, a commune without me . . . as though I'd brought

them together." His last girlfriend, who seemed to have
got his measure, had described him as a "bargain break."

"In the dream I think you are entertaining the idea of
slowing yourself down," I said to him, "but then you
might crash, the pilot might take his hands off the wheel.
And the other fear the dream may be catching up with is
in all the passengers clapping . . . as though this would be
a performance that might make everyone else happy, but
you might think it was absurd . . . the Concorde's made
for speed." His belief had been that the women needed to
get away from him in order to have a chance. A chance of
some kind of concord.

Whether or not dreams are meaningful, they are good
to make meaning with. I was struck by how quickly I
seemed to have a sense of what this man was like, how his
dream seemed so lucid and amusing, without much guile
or anomaly. He made me wonder, for example, whether I
liked him, or whether I was like him. We had struck up
something between us that seemed at first extremely
pleasant. He seemed at once open—and there was a terrible poignancy, a momentary devastation when he talked
about his childhood—and interested in what I had to say.
But he seemed to be reassuring me, as it were, that I had
nothing to offer. He could give me no idea of what it was
about me he might want. I wasn't sure if I was a fashion
accessory or a prosthesis. He might enjoy me as his dream
interpreter—even help me to be rather good at it—but I
would have absolutely no sense what my words were to
him, of what, if anything, he would use them to do. He
had intrigued me, I would discover, as he had his girl-

friends, primarily in order to convince himself that he could escape from their interest. And if this was a patent reversal—that what he was also in flight from was his curiosity about others—he was, among other things, doing what we all do, indeed must do: research into other people's interest in us. But it was only by being elusive that he could create the thing he was most fascinated by, which was fascination itself. Very soon after meeting him his girlfriends couldn't leave him alone. His research program, in the language of his profession, was to work out (or rather work on) the connections between states of aloneness and curiosity; between the solitary self and the desiring self.

"Concorde," he told me with his peculiar archness, in which neither he nor I knew just how knowing he was, "is rather a waste of money, I gather. There's very little room, you know."

THIS MAN OFTEN REFERRED to sex as "a conversation stopper." When we discussed this it was unclear whether his aim in making a pass was to stop the conversation or to fill in the gaps. It had never occurred to him that he suffered—that he could possibly be the kind of man who would suffer—from that most common of conditions: fear of the conversation flagging. What do you do, and why does it matter, when people run out of things to say to each other? If we dread the supply of words between people running out, then we must have very elaborate fantasies about what this currency, this current, can do for us. There was a link in this man's mind between his really extraordinary talent for, as he put it, "keeping the conversation coming and going," and a state of mind, a state of unusual restlessness, in which what he wanted, above all, was something new. He could, he told me, have a room full of books or a fridge full of food, but it was something new, something that wasn't already there, that he craved. This was the theme—like the mood itself—that he would return to.

Keeping the conversation going, I said, always straining to do this, insures that no one can have a new thought, but when you're by yourself it can be exactly the new thing you need.

"The new things, a new start, it's like I want to take off from somewhere else," he said. "If you've already got something, you can never not have it, you can't unknow that you've bought it." (Long pause.) "There's something about the fact that I've chosen it that stops it being new. I've branded it by wanting it."

"So nothing you have or choose is new," I said. "How do you feel about being given presents?"

"I don't like it, it always feels like a vote by proxy, as though something has been taken out of my hands. Just like I never vote because I don't want anyone representing me, I mean how could they, these sound-bitten cunts with their packaged opinions, where are the longshots now, the people with the big ideals who could really poison people with hope, make them want through the roof with their purple passages . . . How did we get on to this? What was the question?"

"How do you feel about being given presents?"

"Someone said if I can think of it, it isn't what I want. Well, for me, if anyone can think of it, it isn't what I want."

"If in this mood you go to a shop," I suggested, "and find, say, a book you want or something a bit unexpected that intrigues you, and it has somehow found its way into that shop, though no one has thought of you . . . thinking of you didn't get it there."

"Yes, exactly, that's what I want," he said. "Something from nowhere, something no one can take any responsibility for."

"So the preconditions are no one has thought about what you wanted and coincidentally you find it. It just happens, with no one having any designs on anyone. But you also seem to be nostalgic for a sort of utopian politics, which means people having very big ideas about what you want."

"What do you do when people who come and see you say they want to have sex with you?"

"You mean when they want to give me sex?"

"What do you do when people who come and see you say they want to have sex with you?"

"I make it clear that that isn't what I do here. But I think it's worth wondering why this has occurred to you now as a question."

"I suppose I'm thinking about the illicit request, how people might want to shock you."

"There's a difference between a surprise and a calculated shock," I said. "Being determined to shock people is a way of faking new experiences. I'd be wondering what they imagined having sex would do for them in the circumstances."

"It might help them," he said.

"It's not the kind of help I want to offer."

"It's odd, isn't it, people wanting to help people . . . it can't help, so to speak, but make one a little suspicious."

"Not wanting to help people might make one equally suspicious," I said, having risen to something.

"But why would you want to help me, or rather what makes you think you can or that it's help that I want?"

"My belief is that you have come here because there is something or various things you want and that wanting itself is confounding you . . . Of course I don't know if I can help you, but from what you've been saying, my wanting to help you, my belief that I have got something you want, already disqualifies me . . . It's as though you can only accept something from someone else if—"

"If they don't think they've got anything . . . That's why in that mood I prefer shops, because they don't think . . . they don't pretend to care about my needs, they let me come across things . . . They're innocent, because they've tried to calculate everybody's wants but no one's in particular, and that makes me free. I can see that."

"Free to do what?" I ask.

"Free not to risk too much . . . free to browse . . . You can't browse people, that's what gays have got over us. They can cruise . . . Cruising is the greatest invention of the twentieth century, and it really will be when everyone can do it . . . It's like nature, really going back to nature and changing the game."

"The game being?"

"Seasons," he replied. "Seasons and children."

"Would cruising be good for you because you'd be free to make choices or free not to?"

"Both. Of course both. If the world's a shop, let's call it a day and shop."

"Or we could try and work out what we can shop for and what we can't," I said. "I think there's something almost being said here, but it's baffled by you trying to make us into a cynical little gang . . . I think your cynicism is distracting us with clichés."

"That's very interesting, that's good, it *is* a cliché, but this cynicism gets close to something . . . It was my father's cover story . . . He could get away with saying things with it . . . There's something sad about this . . . or silly . . . or . . ."

"It takes the risk out of saying certain things, it meant he was exposed in the way he wanted to be exposed. For some reason I'm thinking of your father as a once very embarrassable man . . . and you knowing something about this, you picking this up, joining him without realizing it in some kind of coverup in something being a shame."

"It has to do with claiming things, with making claims for yourself . . . I think all his assumptions about himself were somehow fouled up. I remember the only piece of wisdom he ever gave me—I may have told you this—it was always a joke, the only bit of wisdom my ex-father ever gave me, you're old a lot longer than you're young . . . There are, I imagine, more enlightening things a father might say to a son."

"I think it's rather an interesting remark," I said. "What did you say?"

"I said that all the people I admired had died young, that people who had real lives—I was seventeen—all the people who had real lives, Sidney, Keats, Hamlet, weren't taken in by the wisdom of age, which everyone knew was the second prize . . . and so on."

I THOUGHT THERE WAS something in this man that had no regard whatsoever for the things that mattered most to him. It was like a voice, or rather a tone of voice, that sneered at what he believed—or was so quickly spiteful when belief was ventured—so he couldn't develop certain ideas inside him, or between himself and other people. And because there was a voice inside him that envied his principles, that envied the idea of principle, his integrity could put him at mortal risk. To care for himself he had to be seen to be more or less careless, in a self-appointed solitary confinement.

"THERE WAS A BOY at school—I've often thought of him—who used to wrap his turds up in silver paper and throw them in dustbins. What do you make of that, doctor? Sometimes he would carry one around with him in his pencil case, just in case, he'd say, but the amazing thing about it was how quickly we all got used to it. Just like some people had red hair or big cocks or young parents, he was the boy who wrapped his turds. Discuss."

"I'm sure we could probably both make quite a lot of this," I said. "But listening to it now, what about that story, that boy, puzzles you."

"What puzzles me is the obvious thing about problems . . . When I said that I could feel something shrieking inside me and I could see the mouth all throat . . ."

"Perhaps there's some buried terror in that story, a reason it's stayed with you."

"Perhaps," he said, "but I'm thinking now about another boy at school who had a sister who was disabled, writhing around in a wheelchair, she was there at half-term, and all the family behaved as if it was the most normal thing in the world."

"You know, your saying this makes me wonder," I said, "whether there is something about your own . . . your self that you've never quite been able to come to any terms with . . . that at your best you've been able to enjoy and cultivate an eccentricity, but at its worst it feels like there's something else there, something else going on."

"Like what?" he asked, unnerved as we both were by whatever this was.

"A part of you that feels like it really doesn't fit in, or a part of you you can't do anything with."

"These were boys who had sacrificed their dignity. They . . . had absolutely refused to be or to want to be at all perfect . . . they'd given up that possibility right from the beginning. That boy's whole life started from the premise that his sister was spastic and it was one thing he would never pretend was other than it was . . . I don't start from anything real. I've always got my phantom limbs available, I can go in through the out door, I need to think of myself as . . . optional . . . having options."

"You're crediting these boys with a kind of honesty," I said.

"Yes, but honesty has to be optional, doesn't it? Otherwise it's something else . . . optional extras."

I interrupted to point out that this had already been mocked, there was nothing left of it.

"Why so plaintive?" he asked.

IN THE MYTH, Daedalus was both a criminal and, in a rather more literal sense than Houdini, an escape artist. He was an innovative craftsman who apprenticed his sister's son, Talus, and then murdered him through envy of his talent. Condemned to death for this murder by the Supreme Athenian tribunal, he fled to Crete, where his reputation as an artist—though presumably not as a murderous rival—gained him the friendship and patronage of King Minos. He made a famous and astonishing wooden cow for Minos's wife, Pasiphaë; and when she gave birth to the terrible Minotaur, Daedalus constructed the infamous labyrinth, in which the monster was kept. But the birth of the Minotaur was the consequence—like so many of the mythical catastrophes—of an attempt to evade the gods, to escape from a fundamental obligation.

As Minos offered up a sacrifice to Poseidon, he prayed that a bull might come from the sea as a sign that he would be king; and he promised, in return for the sign, that he would sacrifice the bull. The bull duly appeared, on cue as it were, and Minos became king of Crete. But he was so fascinated by the beauty of the bull that he couldn't sacrifice it, but used another bull instead. As with Daedalus, something about beauty was the cause of his crime. Daedalus's was a sin of commission, he couldn't bear the beauty of the objects produced by his nephew, so he murdered the source. Minos couldn't bear a world without the bull, so he committed a sin of omission. The Minotaur was born of the bull and his wife Pasiphaë.

The story, like most stories, turns on a crucial avoidance. Daedalus is commissioned to design the archetypal labyrinth—the mother of all mazes, in which escape is turned into a pastime, and in which the only thing to escape is the maze itself or one's bewildered self—for Minos's divinely ordained punishment. The artist (and murderer, and successful escapee) becomes the architect of what is supposed to be the perfect confinement. Daedalus is recruited, that is to say, by Minos, to get him off the hook, to become his accomplice against the justice of the gods. He will become, as he attempts, in turn, his flight from Minos, to make himself and his son, Icarus, the rivals of the gods by learning how to fly. Daedalus, in other words, is the archetypal escape artist. And the story of Icarus becomes our instructive parable of taking flight.

What is striking about the story of Icarus—as told in

Ovid's *Metamorphoses,* and retold in later translations—
is the ways in which it is moralized, as though it was
designed as a moral fable, with a lesson beyond interpretation. Or in which the interpretation is obvious.
So when Daedalus in his turn flees with his son from
Minos through actual flight—on wings made of gathered
feathers—it is excessive ambition that he warns Icarus to
beware of:

> Be sure that in the middle course thou run.
> Dank seas will clog the wings that lowly fly:
> The sun will burn them if thou soar'st too high.
>> *(translated by George Sandys)*

It is the middle way, the excessive father counsels
the son, that will prosper. Icarus must neither under-
estimate nor overestimate himself. Escape requires pru-
dential good sense. But Icarus takes such pleasure in
his wings that the means of his escape defeats the end.
The ecstasy of flight makes him forget that he is in flight:

> . . . the boy, much tooke
> With pleasure of his wings, his Guide forsooke:
> And ravisht with desire of Heaven, aloft
> Ascends. The odor-yeelding wax more soft
> By the swift Sunnes vicinitie then grew . . .

In this seventeenth-century translation Icarus falls
from grace, not unlike the arch-heretic Satan, "ravisht
with desire of Heaven." The desire to usurp God or sim-

ply get closer to him by choice or will has an erotic charge (the ambiguity of "desire *of* Heaven" leaving it unclear whether Icarus's is a religious or merely an arrogant zeal). In this Christianized translation, it is the traditional conflict between the individual's pleasure in his wings, with all its sexual connotations, and his faith in his Guide. In a 1703 translation by Lady Chudleigh, the myth has become a rather more worldly parable, the father—ironically, given his own history—reminding his son, and the reader, of their place:

> Ah! wretched Youth, he weeping said,
> Thou'rt now a dire Example made,
> Of those who with ungovern'd Heat
> Aspire to be supremely great:
> Who from obscure Beginnings rise,
> And swoln with Pride, Advice despise;
> Mount up with hast above their Sphere,
> And no superior Pow'rs revere.
>
> O may thy Fall be useful made,
> May it to humbler Thoughts persuade:
> To Men th'avoidless Danger Show
> Of those who fly too high or low;
> Who from the Paths of Virtue stray,
> And keep not in the middle Way:
> Who singe their Wings with heav'nly Fire;
> Amidst their glorious Hopes expire:
> Or with a base and groveling Mind
> Are to the Clods of Earth confin'd.

This, one could say, is a Metamorphosis for the arriviste, like Houdini, a man with self-confessed glorious hopes, and the aspiration—and in his view the achievement—of being supremely great. He was indeed the promoter and the performer of the "avoidless Danger Show": a man famous for his haste, and keen to put his obscure beginnings behind him.

In the more conservative readings of the myth—and it is a story unusually prone to the killjoy, the cautionary reading—it is as though the wish to escape was in itself a transgression. The wish to improve one's position gets its comeuppance. The more obscure question the myth raises is about justice: Which is the more severe crime, the crime committed or the attempt to escape from its consequences? The remoter intimation of the myth is that we transgress *in order to find out if we can escape; to find out just what the servants of justice, the instigators of the law, are made of.*

People would pay, as we shall see, to watch Houdini fall out of the sky, or indeed dropped from a great height. They would adulate him for the superior powers of confinement that he could outwit. Perhaps it was the ultimate luxury for escape to have become a profession, a spectacle and an entertainment. A chosen matter of life and death? It was perhaps the decadence of Houdini— and the culture that nurtured him—that unlike Daedalus and Icarus he had to manufacture things to escape from, that as an absurdist jack-of-both-trades he had to look for things to escape from and invent ways of escaping. And it is not wholly surprising that, like these mythical heroes or antiheroes, he was quickly drawn to flying, to the symbol of modern people's hubris, the airplane. This is what money is now, this is what it pays for in ever more ambitious ventures—spectacular escape. People getting ahead of themselves. People getting away from it all.

"Nowadays I think it will be accepted as self-evident," Michael Balint wrote in 1959,

> that flying dreams and the oceanic feeling (the feeling of at-oneness with the universe) are to be regarded as repetition either of the very early mother-child relationship or of the still earlier intra-uterine existence, during which we were really one with our universe and were really floating in the amniotic fluid with practically no weight to carry.

Flying defies gravity and makes us like gods; flying dreams apparently symbolize a longed-for unity. Either way—whether we go up with the gods or go back to the mother—we lose our sense of insufficiency, of limitation. We escape our mortal bearings (and that weightlessness might also allude to there being no burden of the past). These fabled aspirations and reunions are suggestive because they blur the difference between leaving—home, the earth, one's history, one's mortality—and escaping. Even chosen departures are compounded of things one wants to get away from.

Houdini was uncharacteristically cautious, callow even, when he began to learn how to fly. "I was but a timid bird, and I wanted to take no chances at the start," he said. But characteristically he did think he was a bird, and he knew he would eventually be taking chances. "Aviation," in the words of his biographer Kenneth Silverman, "was for Houdini a made-for-each-other passion."

When Louis Blériot made the first cross-Channel flight on July 25, 1909, Houdini was in England for it. "It was the talk of the world," Houdini said with his usual flair for the large statement, "and made history." Blériot's flight, in other words, was what Houdini wanted to be and to do. There was, he wrote, "magic in flight," but it was a significantly different kind of magic than the magic Houdini traded in. When Houdini took to the air he was, as ever, strapped into a confined space, and would as it were release himself at the other end. And it was the fact that flying was new, and therefore uncertain and risky, that appealed to the Houdini his audience knew; he wasn't the kind of person who would take up flying as a hobby when it was no longer a stunt. And yet his passion for flying signaled the beginning of a transformation for Houdini. He had, for example, made his name by doing things most of his audience wouldn't want to try, let alone be able to do; he didn't want to be imitated, and he did something that people wanted to see but never do. He kept his audience happy to be spectators.

Through his unique—and according to him virtually unprecedented—stunts, he posed a peculiarly modern question: What is an ordeal worth undergoing? His answer was, the one you make for yourself, and that cannot be copied because it depends upon mysterious gifts. And above all, it must not be a once-in-a-lifetime ordeal that changes you. Unlike classical or biblical heroes, Houdini would escape from his self-made, self-imposed bondage, able, simply, to repeat the stunt again. Houdini was a new modern kind of hero because his aim was to be essentially unchanged by his ordeal; he didn't learn anything new in doing what he did, he confirmed his previously acquired knowledge. He had already taught himself the way out; all he had to do was perform it, show it to other people. He was modern man as well-rehearsed man. The only question was, Would what he already knew go on working? And what would he do when it didn't? He was an enigmatic technician of risk. He was not committed in his stunts to making himself (or other people) more mobile, but merely to recovering his normal mobility. If his stunt worked, he was—apart from a little wear and tear—the same person. If his flying worked, he was the same person, but he was somewhere else. Taking up flying was the beginning of Houdini's translation of himself from amazingly safe outlaw to unmasker of those fraudulent transports being marketed by increasingly fashionable and popular mediums. If flying was magic, it was the this-worldly and wholly secular magic of science, a magic that was, by definition, made to be tested and copied. Airplanes had brought the whole mythical notion of flying down to earth.

There were the by-now familiar confinements of modern life—being trapped in work or love, or their absence—and then there was that other modern feeling of getting somewhere, of going places, of progress. Houdini's stunts were more likely to speak to his growing audience about the first half of this modern equation. It wasn't exactly progress, at least as ordinarily conceived, to be able to break out of the best jails in the country, or to get out of boxes that no one was ever likely to get into in the first place. However covert the symbolism, however muffled the echoes that made Houdini's shows so astonishingly successful, it was the magic of no-progress that Houdini was peddling. The message—of course neither perceived nor proclaimed as such—was a consummate and topical irony: *It was possible to do extraordinary things that made no difference.* That to be shocked into disbelief, to be rendered speechless with amazement—to witness the modern sublime of the Great Houdini—had no effect whatsoever. Apart, that is, from the excited wonder produced by the spectacle; but this wonder was an end in itself. Rather like pornography, it seemed only to generate an appetite for more extreme versions of itself. Houdini had to get more daring to make a living, to save his economic life. But flying was different. Flying was progress.

With typical aplomb, Houdini bought an airplane and took it to Australia on a ship. He was hoping to acquire a new title for himself. "I stand a chance," he wrote in a letter home, "of being the First Flier in this country." "I want to be first," he told the Australian press. "I vehemently want to be first . . . it's all I ask." At the same time as he was trying to be first in his new airplane he was also making his Australian debut. He opened in Melbourne, Kenneth Silverman writes,

by leaping from the city's Queens Bridge into the Yarra river, bringing out a crowd estimated at twenty thousand. Several people were nearly killed by a taxicab, and in the crush of straw-hatted men and sunbonneted women straining to see over the bridge, many fell—a "terrible mob," Houdini called it. Clad in a bright blue bathing costume and twenty-five pounds of chain and padlocks, he dived twenty feet from the parapet, head first, into the muddy Yarra, his eyes open all the time to watch for sharks. Billed as "the Great Mysteriarch," he drew large crowds also to the opera house, where he did his straitjacket-Milk-Can turn and revived Metamorphosis.

In this mock-suicide, at once recreational (the blue swimming trunks) and sporty (diving not jumping), Houdini's kitsch flair for multiplying the dangers (height of the bridge, chains, sharks) was the visual equivalent of his boasting. He was the man who had such a way with obstacles that he couldn't get enough of them. And the crowd was so keen to see him they endangered their own lives in a perverse form of imitation. The theme, so to speak, of the event seemed to be people nearly killing themselves for some kind of pleasure. But Houdini was the man who could outwit his suicidal arrangements. There was, after all, no suggestion that he was in a desperate or despairing state; quite the contrary. But he was staging a grotesque parody of a suicidal act. The whole scene was a curious clash of festivity and madness as entertainment. Houdini was performing another of his jarring occasions, in which the knack was to make the spectacle so absorbing that no one bothered (or dared) to be a spectator of the spectators, to reflect on what everyone was up to (Houdini knew what the word "mob" meant). The opera house seemed just the right place for Houdini, just the place to do a trick with straitjackets. "I am submerged in a large can that has been filled with water" (freezing water), as he described one of the earlier versions of the straitjacket-Milk-Can turn, "and the lid is placed on, and locked with six padlocks, and in three minutes I am free. It is a fine looking trick, and almost defies detection." In his strange escapological poetry, Houdini put together a man, a milk can, and a straitjacket; he connected these apparently disparate things to impress people by fooling them. Like a crime, it was beyond detection; and as usual what Houdini actually said was starkly accurate. It would only absolutely defy detection if he himself didn't know how it was done.

But in Australia Houdini was as busy flying as he was falling. Eventually, after much practicing and much fixing of the engine, Houdini was ready to fly. On that day he managed three brief but successful flights, the first of several he would perform at exhibitions in Australia, and the first opportunity many Australians had had to see such a thing. It was not, though, an uncontested first. A man called Custance had apparently flown before him. "I am the first aviator in Australia," he wrote home to a friend, but with a rueful and disguised qualification: "Sans conteste, je suis la première prestidigitateur qui vole." He was definitely the first magician who had flown—and indeed, the first magician who had flown not by magic.

Even if it is intended for public consumption, boasting is a curiously solitary act, the soliloquy of the uncertain. And yet it can also, by a kind of word magic, create the thing it says, by saying it. Houdini's acts, and not merely the advertisements that announced them, were above all acts of promotion. And he was promoting self-promotion as character-building. It would be misleading, in other words, to patronize Houdini for his wish to be first—"the Napoleon of advertising"—because it was a wish not merely to dominate, but to be alone.

ONE AFTERNOON in his "youth" he had gone to South London to buy some drugs, but he was early for his connection and found himself watching television through a store window. It was cricket, which he likes. Looking around, he saw a man in a suit running towards him, being chased by three policemen. In a "fit of civility," he tripped the man up. Enraged and climbing to his feet, the man shouted, "I'm a detective, you cunt," and he ran on with his policemen.

"I thought afterwards that I must have been mad, a criminal trying to help the police . . . I was so shaken by it I just went home without the drugs . . . It was like a dream."

"If it had been a dream," I said, "then you were looking for a policeman, a strong man you couldn't trip up."

86

There was quite a long silence. Then he asked me, half-mockingly, "Do you think wanking's radical?"

"Radical as in—?"

"When I was at school," he replied—he had been at what he called a Sergeant Major Public School—"I had a friend who was a Maoist . . . He believed the only way we could bring down the system would be to restrict sex to masturbation, by law, and then everyone would start really thinking about how much they can't actually do anything by themselves, everyone would discover that they were really communists. They'd want to go out into the fields together, read in groups, all that sort of thing."

I said something like: This is what I'm thinking, but it's a jumble. Mao was a "strong man" who got a lot of young people going, but a lot of people were criminalized along the way . . . It's as if you were trying to find a good strong justification for masturbation, which felt criminal then . . . I was wondering if it felt like a drug, whether it was a good mood shifter for you then . . . but also that you have always been wanting to find out something about your solitude, what you're like when you are alone or even what other people are like, what they actually do by themselves when you're not looking at them.

He said that he'd thought once of writing a story about a man who stays in someone's house and comes down the following morning and tells the couple that unfortunately he overheard what they were saying in the bathroom after he'd gone to bed. And they were such guilty people that they confessed to what they really thought about him, until they suddenly remembered that they hadn't been in the bathroom together that night, that they hadn't talked about him at all that night after he had gone to bed, and that in fact they really liked him, and had been wanting to say this to him.

"I am always terrified when I go through customs," he said. "I think I'm going to faint, or blurt something out, or ask them to take several other crimes into consideration."

"So what's the contraband?" I ask.

"There isn't any, the secret is that there are no secrets, I've got really nothing to declare, nothing to say even." It was like a plea, and he had surprised himself, discomfited himself, by just how frantic he had suddenly felt in this telling.

When he was at school he and his friends had started sending each other postcards during term time, as though they were in fact away. They called them wish-I-was-here cards. Boarding school, he thought, had "opened up a vein of mockery" in him that had saved his life. His father's parents had been missionaries in China, and the tradition in the family was that the boys—he was an only child—were "sent away." His mockery had protected him from an always lurking and chronic homesickness at first, and then it became the currency between him and his friends. The friends would dream up pieces they wanted to write for the school magazine—Dostoevsky Goes to Eton, How to Undress a Superior, and so on—and be "generally literary" together. At school he had obviously come to a kind of life, having been a timid younger boy, and he was at his most animated telling stories about it. It was as if we had been there together and were reminiscing. School had been the first place he could remember missing as an adult. Indeed, it re-created itself inside him so powerfully as he spoke about it that he found himself writing spoofs to me—a bit like wish-I-was-here cards—between times, some of which he showed me with a kind of arrogant embarrassment. They were, he told me, his cartoons. He did not know why he had written them, other than that he simply wrote things; and he conceived of them either grandiosely as part of some far larger, more ambitious "work," or as rather artful and therefore shameful "private eyes." The showing of himself to other people—what he wanted to show of himself, and what people could see without his showing them—had always been troubling for him. He and his friends at school would refer to the books they admired as "evidence."

We talked at—to both of us—tedious length about whether he should show me his cartoons, which sounded in his oblique descriptions of them as though they were either wholly puerile or profound and incisive meditations. It was as though he could never let anyone, including himself, be sure which genre he was in. But at one point he referred to these "works" as "high-core porn."

"When you look at porn," I said, "it seems unthinkable either that you yourself could be a pornographic object to someone else or that anyone is looking at you. You know your place, you know where you are with it."

"Are breasts a talent?" he wondered. "Discuss." After a pause he continued, "In the cartoons I'm both people . . .

both of us. You're going on in my mind as I'm doing it . . .
Without you it's better."

The next day he brought me three "specimens," in
which, as he told me, I was called Nap (Pan backwards)
because, in his view, I wanted to sleep him off.

One day Nap was sitting on his chair and a strange man
came in and lay on his couch. And the stranger didn't
say anything. So after a little while Nap said, "What
kind of silence is this?" And the stranger said, "One you
can't hear." And Nap, who was not put in his place by
this, said, "What is it that you are telling me that I can't
hear?" And the stranger said, "What?" And Nap said,
lapsing into abstraction as a man in a panic does, "You
are making me feel I have nothing you want, and that
what I have got might hurt you." And the stranger said,
"How did you get to *got*? I don't believe in *got.*" And Nap
couldn't help smiling but he was very sad.

One day Nap was sitting on his chair and a man he recognized came in and lay on his couch. And the man
said, "I've been thinking about what you were saying
yesterday," and Nap felt himself sit up without actually
moving. And the man said, "I won't let anyone soothe
me. I must not be soothed. It is a slope." And Nap said,
"If I soothe you, you don't know what to give me in
return. So you think it must be sex." And the man said,
wondering about the *it,* "What does *return* mean?" And
Nap said, "People coming back . . . for more." And the
man thought and thought and then he left again.

One day Nap was sitting on his chair and a man came in and lay on his couch. And the man said, "A woman came to my house this morning, and when she sat down I told her to take off her blouse and her bra. And we talked and drank." And Nap said, "Did you touch each other?" And the man said, "No, I wanted to keep the suspense in the room." And Nap said, "The suspense about what?" And the man, unusually for him, couldn't answer. He could only not-think about the question. But eventually he said, forcing it out as though a stool, "I like possibility." And Nap said, "What did the woman like?" And the man said, getting too cross for his own good, "Is this an examination?" And Nap said, "Perhaps you wanted the woman to have a good look at your body to make sure it was alright." And the man lost interest, and became silly, and left again.

N.B. One day a man called Nap came and sat down in a strange man's house. And the strange man said to him, "I'm a detective, you cunt."

I told him he could be more lucid and incisively imaginative about me when he had got rid of me. It was as if my presence turned him into a more or less coherent, witty storyteller. I wondered if other people organized him in a particular way, if he experienced them as too demanding whether or not they were actually asking for anything.

"I have my best thoughts when I'm by myself," he said, "but I say the most amusing things when I'm with other people."

"With other people you have invented a character you can be. You arrive script in hand when you're by yourself, you don't have to worry about where your thoughts are coming from."

"When I have sex with people it's a routine," he said, "like Nichols and May."

"So it's two people in your mind entertaining an audience, and then there's the woman . . . The things you write in private are inexhaustibly interesting, but the man you bring to be with a woman seems just fascinatingly dull . . . intriguing maybe, but—"

He interrupted me, something he very rarely did, and said, "Vacant . . . My dick's there or thereabouts, but I'm absent without leave."

"Is that what you're always wanting from a woman, permission to leave?"

"OVER THE WEEKEND I was staying with some friends and I couldn't sleep. I was ranging about the house and I came across this book called *Mencius* . . . the sort of thing my grandfather used to have, the wisdom of the Chinese natives . . . Anyway I leafed through it, as one does, for something that would illuminate my darkness. Actually I always read to find something that will strike me . . . for the quotations, I read books as if they were dictionaries of quotations. It's like the lottery. Anyway I was weary, so I just read a few short ones, which were either exotic banal—'If they treasure pearls and jade they're destined for ruin'—that sort of thing, and a few of them

had that charmed clarity that I love. Mencius said:
" 'There are things people find unbearable. To see that
and use it to understand what makes life bearable—that
is humanity.' "

"How can you remember all this?" I asked.

"I've got a more or less photographic memory. It's
better than having a real one."

"What's a real memory?" I asked.

"Involuntary . . . isn't that what you call it? . . .
anyway"—as if I had merely interrupted his show—"I
read a few more because I was gripped by it, but then
when I went to sleep, I couldn't hold back . . . It was as
though the incentive to get to sleep was to make a mockery of it . . ."

"Of an interest that you and your father actually
share?"

"Maybe," he replied. "Anyway, I dreamed that I went
into a shop to buy a tiepin, and a Chinese man behind
the counter said to me, in that jaunty way people used
to speak in advertisements, 'Wisdom! There's no getting
away from it!' And I said to him, as though in reply, 'But
I don't have any ties.' And I woke up, it was a nightmare,
I felt shrouded in it . . . And then I remembered it was
about the book, about one of the parables . . . I'll send
you it."

I asked him what he liked about the dream.

"It reminds me of the nightmare of having to wear ties
at school. I felt suffocated, it was strangling."

"Strangling what?" I asked, but he was blank to that. I
continued, "Ties are connections to people, and the old

school tie is tradition, something shared between you and your father that's called China. Do you think of wisdom coming from other people or from yourself?"

"I don't think of wisdom," he answered, as though from a great height.

SECTION FIFTEEN OF Mencius's book two tells of an Emperor T'ai, who in ancient times lived in Pin. But, says Mencius, the Ti tribes who were his neighbors kept attacking the emperor's country. "He paid them homage with furs and silks, but didn't escape them. He paid them homage with horses and hounds, but didn't escape them. He paid them homage with pearls and jade, but still didn't escape them." Finally, he called the elders together and told them he was leaving. "Setting out from Pin, he crossed the Liang Mountains, founded a new capital below Ch'i Mountain, and there he settled. What humanity! cried out the people of Pin. We can't lose him! Some people followed him like crowds flocking to market. Others said: This is the land our ancestors watched over. It isn't a question of what we want. We may die defending it, but we can't abandon this land." Choose between these two ways and you will choose well, Mencius says.

What Mencius's translator makes him say is unclear. Are we to choose one of the two alternatives, or the always ambiguous middle way? But it is, like the overt dream, about ties (a tiepin may be old-fashioned but it keeps a tie in place). And about the fact that the only thing one is always escaping from is the past. The hopeful, pragmatic part of the story tells us that it's possible to escape from the people who oppress us; but the other part of the story reminds us that it's never going to be that simple; wherever we go there is always the past. We can change places in a way that we can't change histories. Either it is our duty, if not the very point of our lives, to protect our inheritance (the ancestors), to stand our ground; or it is possible, when necessary to leave, to start a new life. It is posed as a choice between tradition or shopping (crowds flocking to market); between two kinds of necessity, two kinds of sustenance. As though we might have to ask ourselves whether we are better nourished by food or by memories. But it is, Mencius says, a choice. We have to decide what it is we believe we can't escape from. And part of that choice is to wonder what kind of life we will have after we make it.

"I WONDER WHY the dream was a nightmare," I said. "What was it you had to wake yourself up from?"

"The more we talk about it the more I feel sad, even ridiculous," he said. "I'm buying tiepins when I haven't got any ties . . . It makes me think of buying ties like going to a prostitute . . . It's like I'm wanting to control something that doesn't exist that I don't have . . . It's shameful . . . Everyone's doing ridiculous things."

"You may be sick of your mockery . . . how it stops you having ties, but the dream also says something very interesting, something like . . . this is what ancient wisdom is for you . . . tiepins for people without ties."

"Yes," he said, "but wearing ties is showing you've got them . . . It's the showing I don't want to do."

"Why, because it feels like a concession?"

"Yes, something like that . . . It's like a promise . . . like spelling out a future . . . saying something is going on."

WHAT WE COME to believe, what we are persuaded to believe is inescapable in our lives, will be a fateful decision. But it is a decision that can never be finalized, that has to go on being made, because things keep catching up with us. Houdini was a man who made no secret of the fact, throughout his life, that he was devoted to his mother— "the guiding beacon of my life"—and to the memory of his father. Despite the claim of one of his early posters, "Nothing on Earth Can Hold HOUDINI a Prisoner!!!," or the medal he was later given inscribed with the words ETERNAL EVADER, he was a committed husband and son. He was married to the same woman, almost certainly faithfully, for his entire adult life, and they had no children, so he was always just a son and a husband.

Escaping was what he did outside the family and in many ways for the (economic) well-being of that extended family. It wasn't that he couldn't get away from his parents, but that like many immigrants of his generation, he didn't want to. His impulse was to conserve and protect; and though he was always working on new stunts, those stunts showed above all that he could preserve himself in adversity. The stunts would change, but he wouldn't. It was the metamorphosis of his apparatus that he was interested in.

"I am what would be called a Mother's-boy," he acknowledged. "If I do anything I say to myself I wonder if Ma would want me to do this?" This was not so much a confession as an astute definition of what is called a mother's boy. And yet what kind of mother—or what kind of mother did Houdini have in his mind—that would want her son to do the kinds of thing he did? In the light of his chosen profession, his comment is a curious advertisement for his mother. Of course, such wondering as he did could go either way: he might defy what she wanted, and what she wanted might be at odds with what she approved of. But one implication of Houdini's description of himself is that he believed his mother wanted him to risk his life. "He had often brought Celia [his mother] to watch him perform," Kenneth Silverman writes,

> of course no time more revealingly than when he made his first manacled bridge jump in Rochester in 1907. He wanted her to see it, he said, because "I thought some-

thing might happen." It is a remarkable reason, as if by plunging into the grimy canal he could rouse her concern for his welfare and in that command her attention. More remarkable still, considering that he might have killed himself, after the performance he wrote proudly in his diary, "Ma saw me jump!" . . . The extraordinary exclamation identifies probably his sharpest secret spur to applause-getting.

As there would have been very little that she could have done if it did, "I thought something might happen" is an oddly ambiguous remark. What, in other words, did he want her to see? It is, after all, the "jump" that he records her seeing, which, though it may be shorthand for the whole stunt, nevertheless emphasizes that what she saw was the moment of risk and courage, not the moment of successful escape. If Houdini was essentially a man performing his secret—secret knowledge, secret skill, secret strength—he was clearly wanting his mother to recognize something about him. He wanted to command her attention, but exactly what it was he wanted her to attend to is obscure.

What Houdini was exposing, in his unusual profession, was something about what modern people could take pleasure seeing being done to bodies; or what they wanted to see bodies doing to themselves (what economics could do to biology, so to speak). Houdini was showing people—showing his mother as often as possible—new ways the body might be tested, endangered, exploited, or confined. What were people looking for, or looking at, when they saw him perform? What did people want to happen, or fear might happen in these spectacular events? What were they looking forward to on the way to the show? It would be a gripping question—though one perhaps better explored in action rather than words—for Houdini, just what it was that his mother did want him to do, just what it was that the audience expected and wished for when they paid their money, and fell over themselves for a better view.

"I have never spoken to Harry Houdini," a friend remarked after Celia's death, "when he didn't say something about that mother." "I who have laughed at the terrors of death, who have smilingly leaped from high bridges," Houdini wrote with his usual brand of stylized bravado after his mother's death, "received a shock from which I do not think recovery is possible." His most extreme stunts had always been about not dying, about the drama of recovery. Characteristically, what was actually possible was left open—he didn't *think* recovery was possible—so his future heroism was intact. But the link he made between his "dare-devil adventures," his stunts, and his mother's death suggests just how important it was to his sense of himself as an escape artist, to shock himself and other people. What was performed at his shows—or rather, what the audience performed—was the shock from which one could recover. Insofar as he knew what he was doing—and he didn't die doing a stunt but, as we shall see, from someone punching him— Houdini wasn't shocked. He was simply the inventor of shocks.

Until his mother's death his physical recovery was always taken for granted. But Houdini's tie to his father involved him in a different kind of recovery. "Houdini also invested long hours in becoming a serious book collector," his biographer writes.

> The effort was linked in his mind with the past, with "my beloved father, selling his library in old age." He managed to buy back some of the Hebrew works his father had been forced to sell, but did much more than restore what had been lost. Although his magic library had swollen over the years into the largest in America, at least, he advertised in the *New York Evening Post* to increase his holdings:
>
>> As I possess the largest collection (private or public) in the world of material regarding magic, magicians, books, scripts, programmes, spiritualistic effects, documents, steel engravings, catalogues, letters, clippings, automata, am still looking for anything that would embellish my collection on the subject of magic or mysteries.
>>
>> HOUDINI, 394 E. 21 St., Brooklyn, N.Y.

It was not only the actual death of his father, but the death or disappearance of his father's cultural life—his father's tradition, his father's personal past—that haunted Houdini. The wealth born of his own success could go some way to preserving this life. But it wasn't just the father's tradition—the Hebrew books—that Houdini wanted to maintain, it was also the whole idea of

tradition (and countertradition), the whole notion of
the things that mattered to him having a history that
needed to be protected. In boasting the largest collection
of magic memorabilia in the world, he was also advertising, and attempting to legitimate, a tradition antithetical
to his father's. Serious, significant, prestigious things are
collected and kept in libraries (and boasted about). Even
his advertisement announced, in the kind of list Walt
Whitman would have been proud of, just what a complex
discipline magic really was. And it was a tradition, as
Houdini intimated, that included a generous, multimedia
range of objects (or idols and graven images) worth keeping. Keeping such things in a library might be akin to
doing a straitjacket stunt in an opera house. It was, as it
were, a library for the arts of deception, for a kind of
scholarship knowingly intending to mislead, a collection
of things that were all about fooling people, for people in
the business of enjoying tricks. The wholly ingenuous
antic disposition that Houdini was bringing to American
popular culture traded on such peculiar discrepancies.
For Houdini the way to be a good man in a bad time was
to be an honest magician.

H E SEEMED A MAN dogged by his own virtue. He lived as though whatever he did carried with it a haranguing wish to be good, like a voice at his back. He told me that Miles Davis woke up every morning with music in his head, which he could play; and then one morning he woke up and the music had stopped. This had been a kind of catastrophe, "he couldn't get to work any more." One day, the man hoped, he might wake up and the voice would be gone. He knew, he said, that he couldn't slip it off, but he thought—and he had thought about this very intently, from adolescence—that he could do something that could drive it away, make it give up on him, as though it would be somehow relieved to, as though he had been an affront to reasonable goodness. He called this imagining his "immaculate crime."

"You know how some people can spend their whole lives working only because they believe that one day they'll give it all up? It's like that, it keeps me going, I'm like a person who looks forward to holidays."

"What kind of thing is it?" I asked. "How do you imagine it?"

"It's not a picture, it's just an idea . . . an idea of itself, a concept . . . I haven't planned it."

"Maybe another way you keep yourself and it going is to keep it vague . . . to work it out would be a disaster?"

"Yes, that's probably right," he said. "Keep it vague, keep it possible . . . it's a sort of harmless double life."

"Yes, no choices to make. I think ever since childhood you've been looking for somewhere else to live . . . but children never leave, only adults do."

"I remember a scene on television when I was a child . . . a couple were having breakfast in a hotel and their teenage daughter came and joined them and they told her they had something to tell her and they told her they were going to separate. This has haunted me in my stomach ever since . . . I'm, I was absolutely terrified of that happening . . . Why do people always say I've got something to tell you first . . . the fucking drama queens."

"It's terrible as a child living with that hanging over your head, it's like a death sentence, a death of something you can't bear to imagine."

"Just to make a child have to think about that . . . to have to try and work out what would be gone . . . it's a terrible strain . . ." There was a long pause before he continued. "One of my friends who's got children says what he can't stand is the interruption . . . but it may be the point . . . Interruption is not the problem but the point if there's no plan . . . It's only called an interruption because there's a plan."

"You may be wondering something about your parents' plan," I said, "trying to imagine what it was like for them having you . . . what you made a mess of for them or you were told you made a mess of."

"Don't you get bored of this?" he asked, breaking the spell of our conversation.

"You've just interrupted us. You've done what we're talking about, and I was just thinking before you asked me, he never interrupts me, never gets impatient and butts in . . . At that moment you may have been thinking, I'm spoiling his plan, he's got more important things to think about."

"Do you think this does any good?" he persisted.

"I think it's good to see where your thoughts take you, to say the things you don't know you're thinking about."

"Give them a run for their money . . . my money . . . When you said that I had a picture of going to the dogs with my father . . . He liked seeing the workers at play . . . He hated his own class, he thought they were the wrong class of people . . . You know my father only ever gave me one piece of wisdom in my whole life . . . You're old a lot longer than you're young, he told me . . . You're old a lot longer than you're young . . . He wasn't, actually, but that's an incidental detail."

"I think you affect a disdain for your father that you don't always feel," I said, somehow riled. "I get the impression that going to the dogs with your father was more than you both going to the dogs."

"My father was a very good-looking man ... very good-looking ... He was like a sex object to me ... I would watch him having baths and it was like being hypnotized ... His chest was like a country."

I said that I thought he might have come up with the idea when he was a child that being good was a way of keeping his parents together. It was like magic, or holding his breath. All he had to do was not be too much trouble, keep more or less on the right side of the law, and they wouldn't separate. But this had made him rather frantic, because he couldn't be good all the time, it was impossible. So he was in a complicated bind: if he was good, his parents wouldn't divorce, but to be bad was therefore a catastrophe (it brought with it a terrifying excitement, a mad glee). He was enraged about being "good" because it was hard work, and he was doing somebody else's job (what his parents did together didn't have to be up to him). This had left him with a belief that eventually he would have been sufficiently good—done enough good works—to finally secure his parents' marriage; and then he would be able to start on his own life. He had wanted to get them to a position where he could take them for granted, so he could stop thinking about them and see what else he might have to think about.

But it was precisely this predicament that had left him with an abiding temptation: the temptation to see how bad he could be. After all, if he could be really bad, "truly evil," and his parents still stayed together, he would cure himself of his superstition. The longer he went on trying to be good, the longer he sustained the belief that it was only his goodness that was holding them together. His good self was a reassurance, but all his goodness could do was inspire him to keep being good; whereas every evil act could be his last. If he could find the immaculate crime—really put the parents' marriage to the test—and get away with it, he would be at last free. Getting away with it meant either the parents were passionately united in their punishment of him, or they were nonchalant about the crime, but apparently more than happy together.

Keeping couples together is a thankless task. As an adult it was almost as if he coupled in order to test the couple. (People become demonic when they believe that havoc is a necessity.) He was, in one sense, more virtuous than he realized, and therefore right to feel quite so tyrannized by his goodness; he was, after all, only creating havoc in order to find out what would survive it. Whatever was left would be something he could really trust. The only way to really find out how sane someone is is to try and drive them mad. He was looking for the resilience, the convincing generosities, in the women he despoiled. His unconscious assumption was that the best thing he could do for a woman he loved—indeed, the wish to do this was a sign of love for him, this was how he knew a woman mattered to him—was to behave in a way that would call up the most extreme versions of herself. That would make her, in effect, a caricature of a certain kind of femininity.

It was in fact a minor incident that had brought him to me. Not really his girlfriend, he thought, but "someone else's error of judgment." He had, in the ordinary way of things, sent an article to an academic journal, and it had been unconditionally turned down. There was no personal letter, just the official rejection slip. He was an arrogant and talented man, sufficiently successful by now—he was in his early fifties—to expect his irritations not to come from this direction. He had been left a considerable amount of money by his parents—which he thought had "kept him young, rather too young . . . Is that a concept now, too young?"—and so he referred to his chosen profession as a "pastime." What this incident had proved to him was that there was something about it, or something to do with it, that was unexpectedly serious for him.

"In this culture," he told me, "if academics think you're a bit naive and nonacademics think you're rather pretentious, then you're probably on to something." He wanted to write things that were "wholly realistic but a bit implausible . . . If I'd made *The Seventh Seal* I would have called it a documentary."

He wasn't, I thought, trying to impress me, he was wanting to start from the position that we were more or less on the same wavelength. It was like being recruited for something without being told what it was, or that there was any recruitment procedure (the official word for this would be "collusive," or perhaps "seductive").

"I don't know which is the daunting thing for you," I said, "not being taken on your own terms, or having to spell out your terms. Was it the being rejected, or there being no redress, their not being interested in your reply?"

He thought this over for a moment and said, "I don't think it was either . . . I think it was the possibility that they might not have read it at all, that they had glanced over my name and my title and that had been enough . . . or that they hadn't even needed to do that . . . they had enough stuff already, it was a bad-hair day for the editorial board . . . I don't know."

"This might have hit you so hard because you're on the other end of something that you're more used to doing to other people."

"Like?"

"Like not being attentive enough . . . disregarding whatever people happen to believe they're entitled to. There's no escape from that sort of thing if you're the victim of it." There was a silence, which I went on from. "If this is true, then I expect that this has been done to you before, and so you unwittingly do it to other people like a habit."

"Assuming people's goodness is patronizing," he said sharply.

I asked him if the officious rejection slip had stirred up feelings he could do without.

"On impact . . . when I opened the envelope I felt totally contemptuous . . . enraged but dismissive . . . The rigmarole was I can always send it elsewhere. I could stop writing altogether. It was a tantrum, I could get back at these people, I could devise something . . . but it became a bit frightening. I imagined myself in solitary confinement . . . I saw myself wanting to bang my head against the walls, but the walls were too hard—" He stopped abruptly as if he had been interrupted.

I asked him what he was thinking.

"A thought just cut across me," he said, "came across me . . . I remembered my mother calling me from downstairs and I shouted back, 'I can't come at the moment,' and my father shouted up, 'You should see a doctor.' I must have been about fourteen . . . it must have been the holidays."

"I don't know if you've changed the subject or not."

"It's about release, but I've only just realized this moment what my father meant . . . It's taken me all this time to get the joke . . . Isn't that weird, it's so obvious."

"If you'd got the joke, you would have got the humiliation," I said, "and then you would have had to deal with all that. Your potency, your who-you-want-to-be is under attack."

The day he received the letter he kept doing something in his mind that he called "time-traveling." He would obsessively wish it was the time before he had opened the letter, the time before the person had written it, the time before he'd sent off the article, and so on and on.

"I thought I was going a bit mad . . . It was like wanting to get back to the time before time . . . I kept noticing that that was what I was doing and I couldn't stop the retreat . . . as though I could undo everything that had happened in order, and I kept thinking where will this end, what's the end of this, where would be a good place

to start again from . . . It sounds ridiculous now but it was
like someone had given me an order, *Start again,* and I
couldn't find where to start from, they were all trouble
spots . . . My mind had that manic cartoon energy . . . It
was frenzy . . . I was frantic, like women always are, you
know, with so much going on, they need something to
organize them like sex or babies, they need their attention selected. The only way I could stop it, the only thing
that stopped it was the phone, just hearing my girlfriend's
voice calmed me . . ."

"When you got the rejection slip you didn't know
whether you wanted to find a woman or turn into one,"
I said.

"That dread was familiar . . . When I was in it it was
like déjà vu . . . I knew I'd done this before, I'd been in this
state before, but I couldn't remember anything . . ."

"No one can be indifferent to being ignored."

"There isn't any protection from it, there can't be . . .
Once it happens it can't be unhappened . . . It's like being
haunted by someone who wants to forget about you . . .
all the moments when one goes unnoticed."

"There can be a freedom in those moments," I said,
and there was a long silence. It was as though I had
insulted him. "When we're ignored we just collapse back
into our histories, into all the ways we coped . . . The
problem is we get stuck with the ways we try and protect
ourselves from it."

As though woken up, he said, "My mother was always
encouraging me to be more independent, but really she
wanted me to leave her alone."

"Maybe all those difficulties you and your mother had

with each other made you think you could be a better mother for you than she was . . . that you could do it all with your mind and then you'd be such an expert on women into the bargain that you'd never really need one."

"I'm always amazed," he said, "when women say things about me that I've never even thought of . . . I must believe I've already thought everything a woman could think . . . Actually, I don't imagine women having thoughts, I imagine they just speak . . . a lot . . . I don't imagine thoughts going on in their heads . . . I think that women are full but that they have nothing inside them . . ."

"You think a lot about what goes on inside women," I said, "but you can't get a picture of it?"

"Yes . . . I can't . . . If I begin to think that they're not like us, not as cunt-struck as we are . . . I don't know about you but I could never remember the facts of life, only the basics . . . All that biology was a killer . . . It was homework . . . It was in the real sense academic . . . It had absolutely nothing to do with the excitement we had about girls. When you stay in a luxury hotel you don't want to see the plumbing . . ."

"There wouldn't be a hotel if there wasn't a plumbing system."

Then he said, unusually worked up or worked on by something, "Only people who secretly hate pleasure are suspicious of appearances. The project is always to see through to something worse . . . Have you noticed that the suspicious always find something worse behind the scenes? It's never even more pleasurable, more beautiful, more exciting there, it's always distasteful, always disturbing, it kills your appetite, thinking about people in fields . . ."

"All I can see here is how much work goes into keeping these things you know about separate. It's slave labor . . . It makes me wonder whether this pleasure is worth it, how much you believe in it."

"It's good work if you can get it," he said. We were enraged with each other and both, in our different ways, awkward about that.

"It feels like some kind of defeat or concession to take these things seriously," I said, "as if something terrible might happen if you stopped disconnecting these things. When you got the letter a you-who-could-be-ignored was suddenly reconnected with the you that you wanted to be . . . When you meet a woman, the person you want a woman to be is suddenly reconnected with a real person . . . It's too much of a shock."

"I can't see what the big deal is about these shocks you want to sell me, what makes them so good . . . I remember going to the optician when I was young and you had to look through these binocular-like things and put the dog in the cage, the hat in the box, and tell them when you'd done it, and I always used to lie . . . I'd say the hat doesn't want to go into the box today or dogs don't wear hats . . . I'm sure overall it was better for my health not to do what they wanted . . . It was facile . . . The first sinners the child meets are all the people who know what's good for him, i.e. everyone, they're everywhere . . . There's no escape . . . It's called being a child."

"You really believe children are innocent" I said, "that if it wasn't for the grownups children would be fine. If it wasn't for the grownups there'd be no children . . . I think that from a very young age you couldn't forgive your parents for being people . . . The only thing your parents ever stopped you from being was another person."

It occurred to me that I was indeed becoming like one of his girlfriends, that I was being put through his hoops. In one sense I felt much freer to speak my so-called mind—freer to be brash, opinionated, preachy, sincere—but above all, freer to be outrightly persuasive. As though he was inducing me to convert him rather than hear him out. I was, in other words, released from certain official constraints, but released into a curious kind of impatience. I became someone who was trying to get him to see reason. What he called up in me was a kind of quasi-religious personality, someone who could rant with conviction, but someone who was left afterwards strangely unpersuaded by himself, not exactly regretting what was said, but unsure of the point of saying it. He had managed to make me, as if by magic, a kind of passionate irrelevance, far from anything in myself that I might think of as good. Encouraged—unwittingly by him—to be a caricature of my virtues, they seemed like vices. It was like alchemy, but in reverse; just as several of his girlfriends had been left feeling as if they could no longer imagine a person who could desire them. It wasn't that they felt unattractive, but that they felt sexless, erotically blank. I, we, became forceful but impotent, full of ideas, but unalluring. We became informative—indeed, full of insight about him—but we lost our magic. It was a vanishing act.

He would unknowingly conjure up the passionate self of his chosen woman only to exploit it. He could, that is to say, turn people into a caricature of themselves, or show them that passion was another word for bully-ing. Show them the stridency of their wants.

THE PROSTITUTE IS FREE of the one thought that preoccupies her client: she never needs to ask herself whether she desires him. She has to reassure herself that she will be unharmed—intact enough to do the next trick—and so equipped to go on earning her living. The only change she knowingly seeks is to exchange her body for money. And all her clients apparently have the only thing she wants from them, their money; but not all prostitutes have what the client wants, whatever it might be that excites that particular person. In other words, they are subject to different constraints, they have different kinds of mobility in the market. The prostitute may have more options than the client, but there's unlikely to have been much choice in her choice of profession. The client may have had more choice of profession, but may have less of a feeling of choice about his sexual needs. In the hard logic of selling bodies in the marketplace, it becomes increasingly difficult to know what the phrase "freedom of choice" might refer to.

There was, Houdini was keen to establish and always to stress, only one Houdini; you couldn't satisfy the particular appetite for whatever this show was anywhere else. He had—as he would do again and again—patented his product, which was what his body could do that sufficiently excited them to make them pay for it. Like everyone in what would soon become the leisure and entertainment industries—and Houdini was in this respect, as in so many others, not so much a sign of the times but an omen of and for the future—Houdini would find the image of the prostitute shadowing his enterprise. But this would never be an explicit acknowledgment—it would have been an intolerable specter for such a proud man to recognize—so much as an underlying grievance. One can only infer from the nature of his complaints and the shreds of his proffered wisdom what he felt and feared he might be like; who he thought he was living as if he was. He seems to have wavered between two positions, two unwittingly assumed roles in life. He seemed to be living as if he was either a prostitute or a kind of social worker: someone who sold his suffering body for other people's pleasure (and who, in some sense, wanted to do that) or someone who was an unofficial guardian of public morals and morale. Because, before exposing spiritualists, Houdini found another niche for himself, made another name and reputation for himself: helping the police and supporting, in his way, the American war effort. There were services only he could offer, but who was in the greatest need of them? After all, for the master of escapes—the man whom no jail or cuffs could hold—there could be clients everywhere.

The man referred to as "America's Sensational Perplexer" held a mirror up to his audiences that was at once disruptive and reassuring. When he visited Russia in 1903 a character in a contemporary cartoon remarked, "The trick is not bad, but if we knew Houdini's secret of opening locks we could break into safes and good positions without needing to have to pull open the door." Good positions were indeed like safes, and Houdini made his audiences think about what social advancement felt like (you needed magic in that society to get anywhere; you needed a criminal mind). In Germany in 1900 he was compared to Faust; but journalists observed what an ambiguous message Houdini left wherever he went. "These are skills," a Danzig newspaper wrote, "that every burglar would give his life to learn. The Berlin heavies are said to have approached Houdini repeatedly, respectfully asking for private lessons in the art of escape." And yet, like Faust, Houdini seemed to be having it both ways; he was that peculiar thing, an overreacher who was on the side of law and order. "It is not without significance," a Dresden journalist wrote, "for the criminal police to know what level of skill can be attained in opening all kinds of locks without the use of any sort of tool or perceptible external force. . . . In criminal investigation . . . such a science can be of great value."

Whether he was a scientist or an artist, an expert on law enforcement or lawbreaking, an arriviste or a protector of the status quo, it was part of Houdini's magic to make his contradictions seem quite untroubling. What was sensational about this perplexer was that he made all such disagreeables disappear. In a file box he kept, labeled "Advertising Schemes," he stored under "Advert. Stunts" a booklet he had written entitled *How to Bring Up Children*. It opened with the words "Bring them up to see Houdini Performance." His mass appeal suggested that the one thing you didn't need to "see" Houdini was a conventional education.

Indeed, one of the remarkable, one of the marketable things about Houdini was that he was so available. Almost everything about him could be used by people to satisfy their imaginative needs. He was like a phrase that could be used in virtually any situation. "Ministers of different sects," his biographer Kenneth Silverman writes, "preached on 'Life's Straitjackets,' on 'Houdini and the Art of Getting Out of Things,' or against drink: 'When whiskey ties you up you STAY tied.' " After seeing him do the Water Torture Cell, Woodrow Wilson allegedly said to him, "I envy your ability of escaping out of tight places. Sometimes I wish I were able to do the same." The literary critic Edmund Wilson—another admirer, who was himself a central outsider—described Houdini thus: "Widebrowed and aquiline-nosed, with a cleanness and fitness almost military, he suggests one of those enlarged and idealized busts of Roman consuls or generals." It is a disarming array of tributes to the suggestiveness of Houdini's image, to the uncertainty he inspired as to whether he was reputable or disreputable, noble or duplicitous. Without saying so, he could show people just how close, just how muddled up, our virtues and vices could become. His exploitable body was enduringly entertaining— he was listed in *Who's Who* regularly from 1919—but was he, as he was so keen to be, a force for good?

Sentimentality is the prevailing vice of those who have doubts about their own virtue. The sentimental boast of their virtue, only to leave everyone suspicious, wondering whom the joke is on and whether it is all a joke. Excessive in most things, Houdini was especially sentimental, more than willing to traffic in the tackiest kinds of good feeling. During the First World War he staged a "patriotic extravaganza" called Cheer Up, doing Land of Liberty Pageants interspersed with the Vanishing Elephant stunt and his Underwater Box Escape. In the words of *Billboard* magazine, he was "entertaining soldiers and sailors," doing extra shows at military bases, and raising money for the war effort. But of course his stunts had their uses beyond simple entertainment. Houdini could cheer you up, but he could also get you out. With thousands of soldiers and sailors leaving each week for France, Houdini, Kenneth Silverman tells us,

> wrote to Secretary of War Newton D. Baker, offering to teach them methods of escaping from torpedoed vessels—techniques for staying alive underwater, disentangling cables and broken pipes, forcing locked latches. A room was fitted up at the Hippodrome [a

theater in New York] to which, by telephoning in advance, officers could bring their men for tutoring during the intermission [of Houdini's shows]. According to *Billboard* the crash course was "daily besieged by hosts of boys in khaki." Houdini taught them how to escape German handcuffs, too, should they become prisoners of war. . . . It probably represented the only time in his life when Houdini willingly shared with laymen, or with anyone else, some of his select, authentic secrets. "I don't have to pick locks for stage purposes any more," he remarked, "for my performance has outgrown those original and small proportions."

His being able to teach these things proved that they were real skills, that the stunts were not rigged. Magic was another word for an illicit talent that in certain circumstances—patriotic ones, say, during wartime—could acquire a sudden, much-wanted legitimacy. Houdini had found safe places to perform his disreputable, saleable talents: first the theater, then the war effort. Circumstances dictated the use value of his skills—what they were good for doing—and the exchange value—what they could be sold for. It was simply a question of the position from which they were described. What was good for a soldier could be bad for a civilian. For Houdini it was a better, but not more lucrative, use of his talents. He didn't have to pick locks on stage any more, but that was also because he had found better stunts to do. Like himself, his audience hungered after the new. The war came at a good time for Houdini because he could share his secrets with "laymen"—not to mention put a few of his fellow magicians out of business—and perform a more obviously socially useful function.

By showing his skills in this way—as he was to do intermittently throughout his life in books and demonstrations—he was helping criminals to outwit the police, but also helping the police to improve their techniques. Locks and handcuffs were exemplary commodities; to keep ahead in the market—to beat their competitors, the criminal fraternity—the police had to be forever refining their tools. Houdini was stimulating the market. Ways of keeping people in and keeping people out were part of a growth market. Houdini was a magician for the modern era; his stunts were all about security. He had to be stopped if people were to sleep soundly in their beds. One of his first business cards says it all:

POSITIVELY

The only Conjurer in the World that Escapes out of all Handcuffs, Leg Shackles, Insane Belts and Strait-Jackets, after being STRIPPED STARK NAKED, mouth sealed up, and thoroughly searched from head to foot, proving he carries no KEYS, SPRINGS, WIRES or other concealed accessories. . . .

under Management of Martin Beck, Chicago

While there are people like this in the world no one is safe. If a man can be stripped naked so that everything can apparently be seen and nothing concealed; if a madman or a criminal, with no gadgets or trickery, can escape from every confining device, then once we stop being intrigued and entertained we might be quite worried. And so, one would hope, would the authorities be. And yet the miracle was that throughout his illustrious life, Houdini was allowed to perform. Indeed, as he would often remark, people couldn't get enough of him. They would only be satisfied when there was nothing left of him. "I created a new line," he wrote, "no-one had ever trod the path of escape until I cut the pathway to fame." It was, as ever, a subtle connection that he was making, perhaps behind his own back: the modern solvent that legitimated everything was fame. He could pioneer the arts of escape just as long as he could make himself famous in the process. Fame was the modern word for permission.

But Houdini seems to have been neither intrigued nor even particularly puzzled by what he evoked in other people. What he was above all keen to do was sustain an audience. To theorize his stunts would have been at odds with his endless reinvention of them. All he needed to know was how to do them, and then how to conceal this information—"mystify" it was his word—from the spectators. What was really going on had to be, to all intents and purposes, what they saw going on. Fame was about making people wonder what, if anything, was hidden, what else there might be that the star wasn't showing us, the secret that might not be a secret. Exploiting what people could see en masse in an orgy of expectant looking made an easy but nevertheless strange demand on the spectators: they had to be both fascinated by what they might not be able to see—Houdini's mysterious "powers," or his sleight of hand—and to forget about it. As with hypnotism (or any kind of seduction), a losing battle with one's critical faculties was being staged. There was the ecstasy, as there is in boasting, of being relieved of one's doubts, released from one's misgivings; and by the simplest, most winning of stories, the impossible obstacle was overcome. In this simple event—dangling, chained upside down, over 150 feet up—the traditional erotic story joined forces with the new economic story: you can make it if you work, if you've got something unique to sell. "The crowds did of course come," his biographer writes,

> the largest that had ever seen him or anyone else perform. Newspapers in city after city tried to gauge their unprecedented size: "There has not been such a crowd of people gathered around a newspaper office in Baltimore since the time of Cleveland's first election, back in 1884." . . . "it was the biggest crowd ever assembled in Washington at one place except for the inauguration of a President." Photographs and films of these gasping assemblies record how much of his success Houdini owed to the mass culture of the new century. The impersonal newspaper offices or bank buildings from which he dangled made a stage on which he could be seen for blocks, playing out a personal drama before a corporate background that he transformed into a spellbinding civic theatre of thrills.

Where once there had been politics, now there was a dangling man. It was like an image the culture might have dreamed up for itself, but with the crudest of contemporary symbols: the crowd, the bank, the newspaper, the cameras, the hysteria, the chains, the upside-down man. And the interpretations of the dream—the readings of the scene—might be even more crass than the symbols it used. That also perhaps was Houdini's magic, that it was the art of the obvious, as though the only thing one could do with Houdini was to be amazed by him (but never amazed that you were amazed). Initially you might want to see through him—and he would include this in his act, inviting you to have a good look— but very quickly that wish would be forgotten, dispelled, only to be replaced by a host of rather more obscure wishes, wishes in which one gasped and screamed.

H E WAS APPARENTLY a rather easygoing man, but with a very definite agenda. He wanted, he said, someone to supervise his self-analysis. He believed, he told me, that when people look inside themselves they only repeat themselves, but when they look out they can see how various things are. He did not want an "introspection lesson," he wanted straightforwardly to solve a particular problem. I agreed to (and with) all this, but with one reservation: that I wanted to be free to say what I happened to think about what he said; that I was not interested in spending my time as an onlooker. It seemed a strange word to have used, but right from the start he produced a stridency in me, a self-assertion that was oddly pleasurable. He had told me to keep quiet, and made me want to show off.

"Yes, because I never did a thing like this before . . . I wouldn't have wanted to for the obvious reasons but I know I'm sick of something . . . of the way I behave . . . It's so childish to say this, to say it like this, and even though I know what you're going to say and you're probably right and probably wrong but I'm like a fugitive now . . . I can't settle to anything . . . I'm always being interrupted, but there's nothing to interrupt, because I'm not really doing anything . . . I've always been able to look forward to the next woman, to the prospect . . . of what she might be like, but that's gone . . ."

"What was it about women that you used to like?" I asked.

"What do you mean?"

"What did you like doing with them? What did you look forward to when you went to see a woman?"

"When I was slightly drunk in the evening I would look forward to the moment I actually made a move . . . when I made something happen . . . When you translate the conversation . . . it's never the same after that."

"Never the same as in it's all down hill, or that you do something that definitively changes things for better or for worse?"

"Both probably . . . When you make a pass you produce a rabbit out of a hat . . . It's like stage fright, you're waiting to come on . . . you're not really there until you come on, until you declare yourself . . ."

"Does anyone you know wear hats?"

He thought for a moment, going along with it. "No, why?"

"For some reason the question crossed my mind."

After a long pause he told me about the letter rejecting his article, an event he would return to again and again, "the scene of the crime," as he called it. I wondered if part of the shock had been that they had rejected the article without hesitation, he had been the victim of a decisive act. This seemed to calm the flurry of words, and after quite a lot of what looked like reflection, he said that he thought something about hesitation was the problem.

"I like risks," he said, "but I can't bear the run-up to them."

"Is an erection a risk?"

"What a weird thing to say," he replied huffily, as though the question was an affront to good taste.

"I'm thinking about the buildup, the foreplay . . . I'm imagining with women you have a very definite agenda . . . that you behave as though you're a man who knows what he wants, as a shortcut around the hesitation."

"Yes," he said, "the women I'm with always complain that I walk too fast, they're always having to catch up."

"Like children."

"Yes, just like children . . . I'm very good with menus, very speedy . . . My mother used to say that I had X-ray eyes, that I knew what I wanted before I opened the menu."

"But what was all the hurry about?" I asked, thinking that they must have been hotel menus if they had covers, and having in my mind an idyllic late-lunch scene, the family poring over their menus in some stuffy grand English hotel.

"Knowing what you want saves time," he said.

"Yes but then you have to wait for the others . . . Perhaps you keep staging situations in which you have to wait . . . Maybe you thrive on all this suspense and impatience?"

"No no, I hate it . . . I hate the waiting around for things to start . . . I like keeping things going . . ."

"Knowing what you want stops you finding out what you want," I said.

"The wait-and-see school . . . Didn't Marilyn Monroe say that any woman who says she doesn't like being grabbed is lying? When I heard that I felt like I was being tipped off, that I'd really learned something . . . But now I'm thinking why was she in such a hurry to give herself away? . . . It's like sharing trade secrets . . . so to speak."

"Once you know that, it gives you permission, you can fast-forward yourself," I said. "What's her trade?"

"Women trade in sex," he said with assurance.

"So now women are the ones who know what they want . . . There has to be someone somewhere who's really decisive."

"Everybody really knows when their head hits the pillow at night what they're looking forward to . . . That's not it for me . . . It's those moments before I make my speech . . ."

The situation that he feared he would compulsively seek out; but not because he was ordinarily fearful of his desire for a woman (though this was also true). It was rather that there was something in that moment—in that seemingly endless suspense before acting—that he wanted. There was something about being in that state that he also desired, and would flee from before he could find out what it might be. At worst the woman was merely the precondition for getting himself into this state. And the trap was that, insofar as it was that prelude to speech and action that he wanted, both the available solutions threatened to come to the same thing. Whether he made a pass (told the woman what it was he wanted) or fled, either way he had merely vacated the spot.

What was at stake for him was not so much risk taking as the experiencing of the risk. He could bring the drama to climax—of fight or flight, as it were—but he was merely ridding himself of the drama. It was anticipation itself that had become a phobic object, because it ushered him towards a threshold of action. Between waiting and wanting and doing something about it there was a terror, a delay that seemed unbearable. There was a Jekyll of definite intent, and a Hyde fobbing him off with either satisfaction—the kiss "planted" as he would say—or evasion, the hurried (and harried) rush home.

I told him that I couldn't work out whether, for some reason, he had never evolved any good delaying tactics, or whether he thought of delay and hesitation—and pausing, which was notably absent in his talking to me—as an affront to his picture of himself. So he was actually in a kind of envious rage with those people who had so ruthlessly rejected his article. It looked like he was fleeing from the woman, or from his wanting her, but it could also be that he couldn't bear to see himself as indecisive. That indecision—a long hovering over alternatives—was not thought of by him as productive. He couldn't let himself be in whatever the state is before choice making. He didn't want there to be any preliminaries. He believed, like the "existential heroes" he had admired as an adolescent, that he was his choices; that decision making was like magic, it conjured a self out of nothing. Before the moment of choice, before the knowing what he wanted, he was absent. Back behind the moment of choice there was a void, which a self had to be invented to fly from. His flight, in other words, was from a state either of not wanting or of not knowing—not being able to formulate what he might want. A pandemonium of inclinations. So desiring was always premature, always rushed through; wanting had become the only escape from not wanting. He once said he was like someone who robs letters from the postman because he didn't get any mail.

I thought that what he might discover if he could hold himself in that moment—stop being a man grabbing things off the supermarket shelves—was his supposed desire disintegrating; he would discover that he wasn't quite so certain about what he wanted, or even *if* he wanted. And since he recognized himself as the person with fast certainties, this might feel like an unraveling, a black hole in which he would be flustered. But he might also discover that this disarray that so haunted him would make some space for the other person to want something; it would let the woman out and into the situation (it would no longer be what he called "one man and his doll"). The terror here, though, was that he could never imagine being influenced, but only usurped; if he was uncertain, the woman would rush in and take over.

The basic scenario was one person—usually the woman, whom he dreaded turning into—as unsure, formless, pliable, not knowing what if anything she liked—and another person, preferably him, of immense conviction and precisely formulated appetite (this person, if a child, would be called faddy, and if an adult, would be called, by some people, a pervert). That he needed to keep it so polarized, and that he lived as though this was the entire repertoire—one way or another everyone in the world could only be in one of these two positions—suggested to me that each was being used as a refuge from the other one. Instead of being able to move between (and through) these options (and into others), they had to be maintained in stark isolation. Ideally the woman would be seen as, cast as, vague in her wanting, and he would be clear. Whether he could actually carry it out was secondary—fight or flight, engagement or evasion, could become virtually indistinguishable; the real thing was the known plan, the fact that there was a prepared move whether or not he was up to it. The actual woman too was secondary, sometimes merely a prop in the drama. Speed was of the essence, because all he needed to see of himself, in his mind's eye, was that he was being a man with a project; a man with a mission to see himself as a man with a mission. Like an anti-Buddhist, he needed a world with his desire in it, confirmed by witnesses. His desire collected him into a picture of himself. The idea, for example, that it might take years for something to crystallize inside him was anathema to him.

I WAS ONCE a consultant to the staff of what was then called a school for maladjusted children. Each week I would discuss with the teachers whatever happened to be the problems of the week. One of the issues that continually exercised and divided people was whether the classrooms should be left unlocked when the children were outside during playtime. It was more or less generally agreed that, unsupervised, an unlocked classroom was an invitation, at least for some of those children, to vandalize the place. These children, it was said, needed to be protected from themselves. If nothing else they were likely to steal anything that was left lying around. In one of these always slightly uneasy discussions the deputy head said she could see them "walking off with the lot." "But what if one of the kids wants to put something good into the classroom?" one of the teachers asked. There was, as they say, a stunned silence. "Like what?" somebody asked. And there was immense relief when no one could think of anything.

WHEN PEOPLE WENT to see Houdini they knew exactly what to expect; it was always, however ingenious, more of the same, and that was the point. In the modern way he specialized, he exploited a narrow range of anticipations in his audience, and satisfied them. As with pornography, the audience knew what they would be getting, but they needed a certain amount of variation to sustain their excitement: not a different body, but different props and new positions. In a sense Houdini was to escapism what pornography is to sex; dazzlingly literal, demanding nothing of the consumer but his money and his fascination. Because their arts depend on simplifying rather than complicating what they depict, escape artists, like pornographers, don't want to change their audience, they want to keep it the same; to raise certain expectations, but not to modify them too dramatically. If the market begins to flag, they may have to raise the stakes. Like a child, the businessman and the performer—and Houdini was essentially both—are in the business of holding people's attention.

Houdini needed, like any artist and entrepreneur, to create the audience by which he would be judged; but he also needed to foster an audience by which he wouldn't be judged, in which judgment—the anxious doubts as to whether he could actually do what he proposed to do—would be quickly dispelled. The audience didn't need to suspend their disbelief—this was not a theater, they were seeing a man playing himself—they needed to hold on to the belief in him they had acquired. Real magic is the illusion that there is such a thing as real magic. It is the skillful concealment of the means of deception. Like a joke, a stunt either worked or it didn't. And for a stunt to "work" for the audience, Houdini had to make all the disagreeables disappear, fast. At high speed tragedy would be converted into triumph, all possible accidents would be overcome; Houdini was unharmed, so it had been a harmless pleasure. Once again the audience hadn't murdered him by paying him to risk his life. Its conscience was clear because nothing had actually happened. What it had thrilled to was survival against the odds. But there was still an ambiguity in Houdini's acts—a frisson to be secretly relished—that was part of their mass appeal. Was this show, like so much of the entertainment industry, a simple recreation in which nothing and no one was re-created (transformed) in any way? Or was a potentially dead body being transformed into a living one before people's very eyes? Was Houdini being raised, raising himself, from near-death? Was this the real draw? Houdini knew that what sometimes kept his art exciting was the possibility of his death. Each of his stunts could be the final one; at each of his more death-defying shows the audience was coming to see Houdini for the last time. They might be paying their last respects. This audience that was so keen to be shocked hungered for the irrevocable. They wanted to see Houdini hit the really inescapable thing.

The pornographer, like the escape artist, trades in people's interest in death. For the pornographer works to avert the death of desire. He knows that for some people in the culture—or for some part of everyone in the culture—sexual appetite is a lifeline, a life-support system, that some people are hanging by the thread of their desire, and that everyone might be hanging by this thread but unwilling to acknowledge it (so much work goes into stopping sex from disappearing). The absence of desire and real death, of which the death of desire is a foreshadowing, are the two great hauntings. Houdini would devote his later years to exposing the fraudulence of spiritualists because they peddled immortality. For Houdini, magic being used to call up the dead was a transgression: it exploited people's curiosity.

There were two things Houdini was determined to prove beyond a shadow of a doubt. First, that the dead could not be called up and did not speak. And second, that the spiritualist mediums, who claimed to be able to do such things, were phony magicians whose magic could be exposed as trickery. Only an insider, Houdini insisted, only someone who was a skilled magician himself, would be able to uncover the ruses required for this kind of public outrage, this deliberate misleading of an audience. Houdini wasn't going to let the bad magic of the spiritualists take America by storm. And yet in Houdini's witch hunt there was, inevitably perhaps, a certain amount of self-revelation at work, a certain self-portraiture in this rather frenzied portrayal of others whom he at once distrusted and couldn't help but experience as rivals in the market. If you are selling shock, if you advertise the extraordinary, you never know what your competitors might come up with.

What, after all, is fake magic? Houdini had to answer this question in order to legitimate himself and his art, with which he was wholly identified (his stage name was his name). And his answer, as we shall see, was that fake magic—and in this sense it was like science—was magic that could be publicly disproven, shown to be rigged. Fake magic was making claims that could be falsified; but this, of course, implied something about real magic, about the magic Houdini acknowledged as his own, a magic not to be abjured. Difficult questions were raised by Houdini's answers. Was the bad magician simply insufficiently skilled at deception, in the same way, for example, that a criminal is simply the person who gets caught? Weren't real magicians, like Houdini himself, deceiving the public, or were they simply deceiving it in ways that were harmless, as actors do in the theater? Clearly, more is at stake if your stunt allows my dead mother to speak to me than if I watch you hanging upside down from a bank, over a hundred feet up, escaping from your chains. Some rather fundamental things are at stake, like what can money buy now? What are at least some people really capable of? Are the dead, in some sense, still in life? Entertainment becomes what we are prepared to entertain. The new spiritualists were doing a version of something too close to Houdini's heart. They were making extraordinary claims for themselves. For Houdini this was a boast too far, because the dead were sacred to him.

To boast is to shout down claims of one's inferiority, the vanishing act in which one's shame disappears. It was the boast of Houdini's chosen antagonists that they had triumphed over the silence of the dead; they could release the dead to speak to the living. And by breaching the final barrier the stunts of the mediums smacked of the supernatural. People had found another way of being like gods; the last prisoners had been released. It was life people couldn't escape from, not death as people had feared.

In his early days as a jobbing magician, Houdini, keen as ever to be fashionable, dabbled in a bit of spiritualism. In the 1890s he performed "tent-show seances," but he was dismayed by just how seriously the suggestible audiences regarded these performances. "When I noted the deep earnestness with which my utterances were received . . . I felt that the game had gone far enough, for I most certainly did not relish the idea of treading on the sacred feelings of my admirers" ("treading on the sacred

feelings of my admirers" catches the disdain of the enthusiastic spiritualist for what matters most to his audience).
This was neither the kind of admiration Houdini wanted
nor what he wanted to do with the admiration he got.
But he did always want the admiration of distinguished
people, and it was this that brought on, so to speak, his
late contest with the spiritualist movement.

Sir Arthur Conan Doyle had lost a son in the First
World War. Through a medium named Evan Powell,
he heard his son speak again from the beyond, which
was clearly, at least to Conan Doyle, no longer quite as
beyond as it had seemed (his son had apparently said to
him, in a loud voice, "Forgive"). This, and further com-
munications from the person he now called "my arisen
son," perhaps unsurprisingly made him an evangelical
spiritualist. A believer before, he was now a devotee. After
the devastation of the Great War, spiritualism took off as
one of the few available means of coming to terms with
the catastrophe. If the dead could communicate they
were not quite as lost as they had so overwhelmingly
seemed. The need satisfied by tent-show seances in the
1890s was very different—on a far smaller scale—from what
the postwar mediums had to offer. For Conan Doyle, as
for many of his contemporaries, spiritualism was not
cheap, opportunist magic, but a precious cultural achievement, not so much an art form as a religious vocation. It
helped release people from a kind of shared cosmic grief.
Houdini's need to expose spiritualism as a hoax therefore involved his taking up a complicated moral position:
the quest for truth overriding the quest for consola-

tion. Clearly, and as he well knew, people would not take kindly to his moral high ground. A magician who wanted to stop people from suspending their disbelief, an entertainer who didn't want entertainment to be given a bad name, was taking a big risk. As a social reformer-cum-scientist Houdini wanted to release people from what he considered were pernicious false beliefs.

Houdini had apparently always admired Conan Doyle. He sent him a copy of one of his books when he was performing in England, a book with the characteristically challenging title *The Unmasking of Robert Houdin*. The masked can be great unmaskers, and this particular book was one of several on a similar theme that Houdini published during his career. In his earliest days as a magician he hawked his own twenty-five-cent pitchbook with the ingenious title *Mysterious Harry Houdini: Requiring no Practice or Special Apparatus* (after reading the book Houdini would presumably not be quite as mysterious). These books, which were about, whatever else they were about, Houdini's ambivalence about mystery itself, were his helpful attempt—not unlike his father's rabbinic teachings—to explain the apparently inexplicable. If there was a malicious side to it, it was at least explicitly self-aggrandizing. Houdini would be the unmasker that no one could unmask; his name would depend upon this.

In the book that Houdini sent there was something that had annoyed Conan Doyle, and that he took issue with. Houdini had reported that one of the Davenport Brothers—famous nineteenth-century medium-magicians who had performed escape acts and spiritualism—had once said that "all their work was skillful manipulation and not spiritualist manifestations." Doyle, like every acolyte, had his well-prepared defense: "As to Spiritualist Confessions," he wrote, "they are all nonsense. Every medium is said to have 'confessed,' and it is an old trick of the opposition." That there was an opposition, and that it already had old tricks, was a reflection of what convinced spiritualists like Doyle had been up against. Houdini, at first, wanted to appease, to be accommodating, but as Doyle became zealous to convert him, so too did Houdini. What had begun as an apparently minor disagreement would become a long and damaging feud.

They corresponded feverishly (ten letters in two weeks). Doyle arranged for the magician to go to seances. Houdini was clearly flattered by the attention of such a great man—"just as nice and sweet as any mortal I have ever been near," as Houdini called him in his strangely expressive language—but rather amazed by Lord and Lady Doyle's credulity. "They believe implicitly in Spiritualism," he wrote in his diary after a stay at Windelsham, their Sussex estate. "No possible chance for trickery." Houdini's reticent and respectful skepticism was met by Doyle's insistent wish to change, or to prepare, Houdini's mind. He must, he told Houdini—whose magic he and Lady Doyle so much admired—attend a seance in a receptive state: "It wants to be approached not in the spirit of a detective approaching a suspect, but in that of a humble, religious soul, yearning for help and comfort." Unlike Holmes or Watson—the detectives who had made

Doyle's name—he must approach this experience rather like a (presumably Christian) novitiate. But such passivity was not Houdini's way. None of the various mediums Doyle sent him to, many of whom were highly regarded, made any impression on his disbelief ("this is ridiculous stuff," he notes on one occasion; "my belief she [the medium] was afraid of me," on another).

As an experienced magician Houdini knew all the tricks. And this was particularly galling for Doyle because he believed Houdini himself to have such supernatural powers: "why go around the world seeking a demonstration of the occult when you are giving one all the time. . . . My reason tells me you have this wonderful power, for there is no alternative." To Houdini, of course, this would be doubly insulting; he didn't believe in occult powers, and he didn't believe he was like anyone else. After all, if one gave such credit to occult forces, what could one claim for oneself? Where was the real mystery in being merely connected to a higher power or a deeper source? The real modern individualist didn't have to know where his talents came from in order to claim them as his own. He simply had to make their provenance sufficiently enigmatic to be unshareable. Houdini wanted to be a great magician, not the member of a cult; and it was this necessary distinction that became his raison d'être.

In his crusade against spiritualism, which was to ruin his friendship with Conan Doyle, Houdini was becoming the very type among his own audiences he had always needed to disarm: the faultfinder. In devising his remarkable stunts it was the faultfinder in himself that he would always need to silence before he could perform the stunt in public. Once he knew his own most suspicious critic couldn't see through the act, could only see that it had been done but not how it had been done, then it could be shown. Either real magic involved supernatural powers, and the magician was a kind of hieratic figure; or real magic was the ultimate art of concealment, the business in which deception was the name of the game, and in which the audience showed, above all, its willingness to be well deceived. When good magic was performed, when the necessary illusion was created, criticism was replaced by wonder. Just as with pornography—which would soon become the seamier side of the new entertainment business that Houdini was in on the beginning of—one wouldn't bother to read the scene, to interpret what one saw; one would be either excited or not, entranced or appalled. For the audience, in other words, it would be fight, or flight, or consume. Houdini had created an audience for himself that could relax into astonished amazement, that would pay to be unavoidably thrilled and mystified. The spiritualists, he believed, with their quasi-religious legitimacy, were exploiting the audience's credulity in the wrong way. It was a new twist to the old question of how true belief differs from false belief and why it matters. The argument between Doyle and Houdini became predictably contorted.

On a lecture tour in America in 1922 to spread the New Word, the Doyles visited the Houdinis. "Socially," Kenneth Silverman writes, "the afternoon was a success." Houdini pleased Sir Arthur with the gift of a pamphlet that had been given him by Ira Davenport, receiving in turn an inscribed copy of Doyle's *Wanderings of a Spiritualist.* But Doyle said that what interested him most was the trick Houdini showed him in a taxi as he took the Doyles back to their hotel. Houdini apparently removed the first joint of his thumb, showed it separated from the rest, then replaced it. Lady Doyle "nearly fainted," Houdini remarked. "You certainly have very wonderful powers," Sir Arthur wrote him later, "whether inborn or acquired." Doyle's response may have flattered Houdini, but cannot have increased his respect for Doyle's fraud-meter. The detached thumb-joint is kindergarten-level magic that can be done by a five-year-old. "Never having been taught the artifices of conjuring," Houdini noted in a memorandum, "it was the simplest thing in the world for anyone to gain his confidence to hoodwink him."

Houdini's triumph was shadowed by the knowledge that his own success depended upon gaining people's confidence. In the encounter in the taxi, one could say, the magician met his ideal audience. Not the hardheaded empirical scientist, not the vigilant detective who depends for his sense of himself on being foolproof, but the five-year-old child was in the taxi with Houdini. It was all about, as Houdini said, gaining people's confidence to hoodwink them. There were, of course, very few enterprises—including child rearing and magic—that did not involve the gaining of people's confidence. What confidence might be that it could be so gained was the issue. The successful magician, as Houdini clearly knew, trades on the hallowed virtue of trust. Good magic, he seemed to believe, harmlessly exploited people's childlike willingness to believe what they see, to trust in the powers of others. It depended on a rather interesting and surprisingly common wish, the half-conscious wish to put one's trust in the untrustworthy.

Knowing of Houdini's skepticism, Doyle could no longer trust him with his mediums. Doyle would arrange a reputable seance for Houdini to attend, after which the magician would more or less politely explain to Doyle how it was all done, with his insider's knowledge of the artifices of conjuring. "I caught him red-handed," Houdini wrote to Doyle after one such experience with a spiritualist called Reese, who had apparently convinced Thomas Edison of his extraordinary gifts. "[Reese] acknowledged it was the first time in his life that anyone had ever 'recognized his powers.' And I'll put it in writing he was the slickest I've ever seen." This kind of trickery was a criminal act for Houdini, because he could see through it, because its artistry wasn't opaque. And this makes Reese's confirmation even more ironic, because Houdini had recognized that Reese didn't have powers, or if he did, these powers were a kind of illicit skill. What Houdini needed to prove was that there was nothing and no one else there but the magician himself. He had only his own capabilities. They could only be called "powers" if they enlisted no other power than the magicians' under-the-counter technology.

"I have never seen or heard anything that could convince me," Houdini wrote in the *New York Sun,* "that there is a possibility of communication with the loved ones who have gone beyond." Spiritualism was bad magic—its methods were shoddy—and it was in the service, in his view, of something wholly disreputable. But why were the limits of magic so important for Houdini, and why did he draw the line here? Was communicating with loved ones who had gone beyond unacceptable because it was untrue—demonstrably fraudulent—or unbelievable because it was unacceptable? Houdini's misgivings about the spiritualists were not merely the professional indignation of a perfectionist, but rather the determined insistence of a converted man. And in this sense, Doyle and Houdini were mirror images of each other. Houdini was convinced that the dead were unreachable, and that it was a dangerous confidence trick to show otherwise; for Doyle it was a secular heresy to deny that the dead spoke.

Like any successful professional magician—and Houdini was the man who put magic on the map, who took it out of quackery and into mainstream entertainment—Houdini had no appetite for the inexplicable; he wasn't keen to be impressed by it. He didn't claim to understand everything, but what had always fascinated him was people's talent for creating mystery. "Sir Arthur," he once told Doyle, "I have been trained in mystery all my life and every once in a while I see something I cannot account for." But when this happened he wanted to discover how someone had done it. Mystery, for Houdini, was the great secular commodity. When we reach the limits of what people can invent we can start talking more accurately about the beyond. So passionate was Houdini about all these particular issues that he changed his medium, so to speak; he moved from showing to telling, from magic to lecturing on the evils of spiritualism. "Houdini the magician has become Houdini, the educator!" *Billboard* magazine announced.

In 1924 he lectured at universities and public meetings across America about the methods and dangers of fraudulent spiritualists; the spiritualist as merely another word for the charlatan, the exploiter of magic. "Houdini did more than talk," Kenneth Silverman writes. "He established himself as a leading investigator of psychic phenomena." And investigation for Houdini—which was to involve him with many prominent scientists and legal experts, the legitimate, respectable professions—meant proving beyond a shadow of a doubt that there was no such thing as psychic phenomena. It was a crusade to defend the honest deception of magic, and the separation of the living from the dead. As causes go, these were strange bedfellows. Perhaps this was the apotheosis of Houdini's individualism, the ultimate form of self-justification (many of his secrets went to the grave with him, so there were stunts that would never be reproduced). Everyone he could expose was a fake, and he was the real thing because there was no one who could expose him; as if it would take a Houdini to unmask a Houdini. And perhaps the real thing—the real thing for a secular age—was neither to claim nor to invoke psychic phenomena, but only human skills simply beyond disproof. For Houdini the silence of the dead—that the living and the dead are out of reach of each other—was inescapable. Everything else was up for grabs.

For this work on behalf of the public good Houdini would satisfy one of his abiding wishes: to be recognized by the distinguished. Performing exposés of mediums in tests sponsored by *Scientific American,* or corresponding and collaborating with the Harvard University Psychology Department—that "wonderful institution," as Houdini called it—in this line of work Houdini was finally turning his magic skills to reputable account. The wholehearted entertainer had become the uniquely equipped pursuer of truth, and for the good of all. Walter Lippmann, one of America's most highly respected essayists and journalists, praised Houdini "for the work you are doing, resisting superstition and credulity." Houdini may have made his name by trading on credulity, but he had patented more wholesome forms of superstition. In 1924 he published what he described as his "monument," *A Magician Among the Spirits,* a treatise on the scandal of spiritualism. Once again the title had that brash irony that Houdini had made his trademark. A magician could never be among the spirits; the spirits were precisely what the magician dispelled.

The editors of *Scientific American* had justified the inclusion of Houdini on their committee to investigate spiritualist mediums by pointing out that he would be "a guarantee to the public that none of the tricks of his trade have been practiced upon the committee." Like the fabled Universal Acid, these tricks of the trade were clearly uncontainable. Only the great trickster himself could protect the committee from the mysterious pitfalls of their investigation. But how would they know that Houdini wasn't tricking them? Wasn't his very inclusion in the project a parody, or perhaps an emblem of the problem? Was the arch-deceiver the best expert on truth? When it came to the most skillful tricks of the trade, what kind of guarantees were there? What would stop Houdini from being the wrong kind of double agent? It was Houdini's unique but exemplary artfulness to make himself the magician the public could trust. They knew he was brilliant at deceiving people. That's why they could trust him.

The *New York Times*, reporting on the much-publicized investigation in which Houdini and other members of the committee would sit in on seances as participant observers, noted that "Sir Arthur Conan Doyle is a detective after [the spirits'] heart, but a gentleman who knows everything about legerdemain makes them very uncomfortable." Houdini, who wanted to be a gentleman, and to be thought of as knowing everything about magic, was delighted. "A most remarkable compliment," he wrote on his clipping. "Three of the great newspapers of the world The New York Times, New York World and New York Tribune, use Houdini materials and in Editorial. I certainly feel complimented."

Unsurprisingly, though, some of the academics on the committee were as indignant about Houdini's status as the spiritualists. Dr. William McDougall, chairman of the Psychology Department at Harvard, was not enthusiastic about having his expertise confirmed by Houdini. But his protest revealed the absurd ambiguity of Houdini's position, the unofficial importance he had acquired through his life's work. "It makes him seem to have a monopoly of intelligence and of caution," McDougall complained to the press. "I do not require Houdini to teach me something about which I probably know more than he does." But what exactly was it that he knew more about, and what kind of knowledge was this? McDougall was a professor of the relatively new science of psychology, at the most prestigious university in America; Houdini was a practitioner of magic with no institutional affiliations whatsoever. It was a question about what, if anything, could guarantee a point of view as especially trustworthy. Houdini was a shrewd user of the available rhetoric. "Men like Professor McDougall . . . and Conan Doyle are menaces to mankind," he told an interviewer, "because laymen believe them to be as intellectual in all fields as they are in their own particular one." They too, like the spiritualists, gained people's confidence to hoodwink them; there was a new clergy of respectable experts, and everyone else was a layman. To Houdini it was clear that spiritualism, because it was magic, was within his domain. "How can a man trained to deal only with facts," he asked with his curious unentitled assurance, "and whose mind runs along channels of rectitude, hope to cope with an individual whose whole stock in trade is a bag of tricks." He meant the medium, of course, but he was also referring to himself. How can the honest, whose minds run along channels of rectitude, deal with—not understand,

Houdini pointedly says, but cope with—the deceitful? But if, as Houdini asserts, it takes one to know one—only a man with a bag of tricks, only a man who sees himself as essentially a bag of tricks, can recognize one—then the honest, if they are to pursue truth, must be competent at dishonesty.

As moral reform went, this was dangerous logic. To suggest that, say, the good policeman must be an effective criminal, or that the only good psychiatrist is a mad one, may have intuitive appeal, or, indeed, seem obviously true. But what then should they be trained in when the men trained to deal only with facts, the scientific psychologists, are so easily duped? It was as though the voice of Houdini's dead father, the lawyer and rabbi, was being turned upside down; and yet a morality was still being preached and fought for. "When they shout the words 'itinerant magician,' " he told an audience in 1924 after one of his shows, "I want you to come to my home in New York and look at my library." The words mattered. The phrase "itinerant magician" sounded, perhaps, like "wandering Jew," and Houdini had a home. He objected to being called a "magician" in *Who's Who* and requested instead "actor, inventor and author." Those words now were a better description of what he took himself, as a magician, to be.

The man now billed at the New York Hippodrome as the "World-Famous Author, Lecturer, and Acknowledged Head of Mystifiers" was once again, in the very act of self-entitlement that he had needed to make his own, advertising himself as an unusual, though strangely contemporary, combination of talents. He was neither a rabbi, a teacher, nor, by profession, a writer; he was uncredentialed and had a unique and proven talent for deception. And he had created out of words his own consensus about himself.

ALL SYMPTOMS ARE a kind of geography. They take a person in certain directions, to certain places and not to others. They are a schedule of avoidances, a set of warning signals. Whether I am straightforwardly phobic, or obsessive, or unstraightforwardly hysterical, my symptoms map out the limits of my life; I confine myself to particular kinds of situations, I find myself approaching certain kinds of people but wary of certain others. Like anxious parents, my symptoms keep an eye on me; my suffering provides stability. Every second one's entire being is metamorphosing— the cells of the body are destroyed and reproduced at an astonishing rate, in the ongoing push towards final disintegration—but one's experience is that at least in some areas of one's life there is some certainty, some fixity in the turbulent business of living (when it becomes intolerable one feels "stuck," when it is comforting it's called habit). The unavoidable fact of change is apparently countered by the inescapable nature of one's symptoms. There are parts of one's life—one's erotic preoccupations or professional inclinations, over food or leisure—where one just keeps repeating oneself, if not quite literally quoting oneself. So the not always obvious pleasure people take in their symptoms—if only by ironizing themselves as "characters"—always raises the question why, at this moment in their lives, they want to lose such an absorbing and upsetting pastime, to get rid of such an arresting concern?

When someone finally asks for help, their attitude to time (to the time of their life) and to space (the places or situations they can join in) is already changing. The alien symptom is required to become a communication, a useful message, so that it can be recruited for a person's project, and not used to block or sabotage it. There has to be something one wants enough that the symptom baffles, and this obstructiveness must have become insufferable. In other words, a project—something that, for whatever reason, one wants to do—reveals itself as imperative. And this in itself is an acknowledgment that one won't live forever (if I have all the time in the world it doesn't seem to matter when I do anything; and that translates as, it doesn't matter if I do anything). The symptom, in other words, if it works, if it becomes sufficiently unbearable, forces a person to recognize that he has projects. There are certain things that for some reason he really seems to want. The symptom traps one into recognizing what is ultimately inescapable for oneself.

So WHAT DID this man want who, unsurprisingly, given his symptom, would only see me for a short time? On the one hand he wanted to rid himself of a vulnerability that was so starkly prompted by the letter, but that was, as he saw, everywhere in his relations with women. And on the other hand, there was something that puzzled him. He was so thrown by something that kept happening— his need to find women to flee from—that he was at the mercy of his curiosity about himself. The woman as object of desire had been replaced by flight from the woman as an object of desire. As he said, "the moment I find a woman I like I have to get home." He had begun to wonder whether it was home by himself that really appealed; and whether the symptom was merely signaling something he needed to acknowledge, that he was "a happy bachelor," and a poor partner. It was, after all, a familiar dilemma: home by oneself (but with one's parents—in fantasy—because home is where the parents are); or elsewhere, with someone else, out of one's parents' orbit, and out of one's own.

He knew what he called "the litany of the uncommitted" that was endlessly repeated—spoken of, written about, lamented, and enacted—by the people of his class and education: fear of dependence, fear of loss, envy of women, addiction to a male ideal, and so on. None of this was (or is) news that stays news. It was, however, illuminating to him to realize that what he was wanting—that the object of desire that almost literally entranced him—was the image of himself as someone who could get away, who had the wherewithal to escape in one piece. And whatever his fear of women was, it was as nothing compared with his terror of his desire growing inside him. This was the experience he was trying to rush, and it didn't matter in which direction he went. Away from the woman or towards her was the same direction; either way he was "spared," released from the confinement, the suffocation of the feelings that would begin to expand inside him if he stayed in the room with the woman but kept a distance. Anticipation allowed to flourish in its own time, in the presence of a woman he was drawn to, felt toxic, felt like a foreign body. As he said, in his mock-gothic way, "When you want a woman you give birth to a monster."

And so he needed to make a paradoxical demand on me, as he did on anyone when he needed something from them. I was being recruited to make him a better escape artist; to help him come to some "mature," stoically resigned wisdom about himself, to enable him to acknowledge a hard but necessary fact about his fate, that he was probably better off by himself. And yet I was simultaneously being asked to spring him from all this running off; to explain to him the whys and wherefores of his escapades, with the hope that such understanding would release him into a world of choice. The compulsive man would become the decisive man. But my options were then symmetrical with his. And it was this, once I could see it, that revealed the difference between us. He wanted me to turn him into a better choice maker. I wanted to turn him into a better risk taker.

He once told me a story about a woman in a local bookshop whom he had fancied. He would go into the shop and browse, and they would chat about books, and flirt, and rather too obviously amuse each other, to the annoyance of the owner. He thought that they got on rather well, but then he would occasionally notice that she was as easy, as amusing, with several other customers. So how could he tell whether this was just what she was like, or whether there was, as he put it, "something between them." He told all this to a trusted female friend, and she said to him, "Perhaps *she* doesn't know. Women sometimes have to be told what they want and that makes them work out what they might want." Accepting this as oracular advice, he wrote the woman in the bookshop a letter, asking her out for lunch. Then, as he said, "one thing led to another." What had so impressed him about his friend's advice was the idea that you could tell a woman what she wanted.

"I think your friend's advice is more interesting than that," I said. "I think she's saying, tell this woman what she wants and then she can begin to wonder what her wants might be . . . It's not about giving orders, it's about just starting something off."

"No, I don't see it like that at all," he said. "I think you've missed the point."

We seemed to leave it at that. It was characteristic of our way with each other that every so often I would have a very strong sense of the significance of something, which I would be keen to let him know, and it would be met with a kind of irritated indifference. In such situations it was as if the irrelevance of what I had to say was an affront to his intelligence. Any insight that I might have would seem silly.

I had begun to refer to these impatient brush-offs as his "flight into inner superiority whenever he was ruffled." Needless to say, this would then create further flight. On this occasion I just decided to give him a brief lecture. "I think what's important about this story is the idea of someone finding out what they *might* want . . . This is the experience you're always trying to evade . . . the space in which you could find out what you *might* want . . . not your real, deep, authentic desires but your inclinations, your whims, your half-chances . . . that whole repertoire of experiments that you are."

"So you think it's about risks," he said with unusual sheepishness. "Yes, there may be something in that."

"Yes, it's about risks, not choices . . . You're so busy making choices that you never take any risks."

It had seemed to me that something had been said. The following day I received a courteous and quite appreciative letter from him saying that he had found it "unexpectedly interesting," but that he had been thinking for some time that it might be better to stop, and "now seemed as good a time as any." I wrote back disagreeing as agreeably as I could, but heard nothing. I had now received a version of the letter that had so thrown him, and the opposite of the letter he had sent the woman in the bookshop. And I received nothing else from him; except, that is, the thoughts he has left me with.

WHEN IT COMES to the perennial question of what it is we want—and we have only become the people we are because we have wanted—there are, traditionally, two forms of escapism available to us. One can escape into doubt about what one wants, or one can escape *from* doubt about what one wants. These two forms of doubt, these two refuges, coexist in everybody, and are not always easy to tell apart. And even though they are never found in their pure form, people tend, in the ways they actually live their lives, to be escape artists of one kind or another.

People with what psychoanalysts—and other committed moralists—call perversions seem to know exactly what they desire. However shameful or otherwise troubling, their excitement, their engagement, is apparently guaranteed by certain acts or scenarios or kinds of people; to spank or be spanked, to watch or to flash, to urinate on or be urinated on, to be rich, to be beautiful, to be enlightened, to be safe, to be honest (and their opposites). These people know exactly what works for them. They always know beforehand what the object of desire is; they know the aim, even if they don't (yet) know the way. They have what might be called a sense of direction, or even a vocation of sorts. They are narrow but sometimes bright with purpose. Their lives are utterly dependent on their objectives. And they are people who are on the run from a fundamental and unnerving uncertainty about their desires. They can't risk too much questioning of what they want because it would question who they are. They are the fundamentalists of what they take to be their own nature.

It is characteristic of these people that they whole-heartedly recognize themselves in their desires; from their own point of view, they are what they want, and there is virtually nothing else left over. How to do anything other than wanting is inconceivable to them. They are always shopping, and they rely on their quest's being at once endless and perpetually successful. They are often hopeful, in other words, because they believe that if they want something it must be there somewhere; and they will always know it when they find it (it is as though they have already read the story of their lives). So to lose faith that wants are knowable, and therefore potentially satisfiable, amounts to what used to be called an existential crisis. These people live in continual dread that they might forget what they want and how to want it; or that they might even forget that they want. And contemporary culture has acknowledged this fear; there is, for example, clearly widespread panic that we might forget about, or lose interest in, sex, so a lot of work and money goes into keeping at least the idea of sex, the image of it, in circulation.

These people, that is to say, are fleeing from confusion and uncertainty about what they want and whether, in fact, they want anything. Any culture that takes wanting as seriously as ours—that offers so few alternative satisfactions—must be talking itself into something, and out of something else. It must obscure what it might be escaping from by dazzling people with what they might escape to. These people, the people with conviction, are the fashion victims of their time. At their most frightened, what they desire above all is certainty, what they have to be certain about is secondary. For them skepticism is not an easy option, it is a terror.

For the other kind of people—those who are so convinced of what they want they will do anything to obscure it, mystify it, disguise it, sabotage it—their refuge is doubt. When their heads hit their pillows at night, when their minds wander, they know exactly what they are looking forward to in their heart of hearts. It is so obvious, so self-evident that it is a full-time job—an entire life story—to insure that they never get anywhere near their heart's desire. They live in mortal terror of not frustrating themselves. For these people, the faultfinders and ironists, skepticism about what they and everyone else really want—skepticism about whether the phrase "really wanting" means anything—is the easiest, most necessary thing in the world. To avoid their crisis of choice they need to see through everything. The convinced are in flight from the experimental nature of wanting, from the fact that you can only find out what you want by trying to get it, and in the process you may find something else that you hadn't known you wanted. The unsure are in flight from acting on inclination, from following the compass of their excitement. For the unsure there is always a safe haven of compromise, of world-weary wisdom about the impossibility of satisfaction, and the noble truth in disappointment; whereas the convinced live in a different kind of inner superiority, the belief that they really know what everyone really wants, but that they are the only ones with the courage, the recklessness, the moral strength, or the good fortune to be capable of the ultimate satisfactions that life has to offer.

Skepticism is a refuge from conviction, and conviction is a refuge from skepticism. Each is a relief from the tyranny of the other. But these two parts of ourselves that we can play are always envious of each other, and often secretly believe that it is the other who will be saved, the other who just might be the happier one. So they must never meet, never be on speaking terms, because they fear conversion; and for both of them conversion is the only imaginable form of change. Indeed it is their mutual suspicion that sustains and fortifies them. Both of them, in other words, glamorize risk to avoid taking one.

I AM NOT A MAGICIAN," Houdini would often say, "but a mystifier." It was a characteristically mystifying remark, but the distinction was an important one for Houdini. There was, as his quest to expose the spiritualists was meant to confirm, no such thing as magic. And therefore there could be no bona fide magicians, only people with a talent to confound others. Testifying before U.S. Senate and House subcommittees in 1926 to discuss an anti-fortune-telling bill, Houdini was asked by a Mr. Hammer to explain himself:

MR. HAMMER: I didn't understand what your occupation is.
MR. HOUDINI: I am a syndicate writer; I am an author, and I am a mystifier, which means I am an illusionist.
MR. HAMMER: You don't claim to be able to do anything by divine power?

MR. HOUDINI: No, sir; I am human. But mediums are trying
to say I am psychic. That is not true. . . . But I do tricks
nobody can explain.

Houdini's art was the art of the inexplicable. It was his
intention to devise stunts that no one other than he
could explain. To be an illusionist, to be a mystifier, was to
be selling that most reassuring of commodities, the mystery that someone understands. No higher powers, no
divine interventions, just a human being. And of course,
once you take divine power out of the picture, the human
talent seems even more extraordinary. Unassisted people
can make mysteries that can compete with the supernatural, and thus make themselves even more mysterious. If
the illusionist doesn't have a god inside him, what does he
have? When Joyce wrote in *Finnegans Wake* of the "escape-
master-in-chief from all sorts of houdingplaces," he was
referring to the self-made man as self-made mystery.
They were indeed houdingplaces—he had made them;
and it was precisely this that made him escapemaster-
in-chief. One can only be master of something one has
made.

If there are no divine powers involved, then it is only
his body that the mystifier has to contend with. Houdini had made the name that was his living out of self-
imposed challenges to his physical strength and to his
ingenuity. He was always having to imagine and test what
his body was capable of. But these self-imposed stunts
were driven by a market; like a pornographer, he had to
calculate what was at once salable, satisfying, and within

the range of bodily possibility. It had to be sufficiently remote from so-called real-life situations, but at the same time seem strangely familiar. It wasn't difficult for Houdini's audience to see itself and him as both, in their own ways, trapped; but compared to the Houdini it had paid to see, the audience was remarkably safe and free. And what was heroic about Houdini in the popular imagination was that he was a man who thrived on risk. He sought it out; he would, as it were, invest his body in the most difficult situations. This was his pleasure and his power. If, towards what turned out to be the end of his life, Houdini seemed to be returning to his version of his father's world—he thought of going to Columbia University to study English, or starting a school of magic ("Magic, as an art and as a science, will be elevated to a higher level")—it may have been because forty years of this work was taking its toll. If you virtually invent a profession you also have to invent how to grow old within it.

And yet the way Houdini died seems uncannily of a piece with the way he had lived, as a man who could adapt to and master the most absurd demands. One evening in 1926 a young student came to his dressing room to meet him and ask some questions. The student, called Whitehead, Kenneth Silverman writes,

> asked Houdini his opinion of the miracles mentioned in the Bible, and looked taken aback when Houdini declined to comment on "matters of this nature." Then the inquisitive young man began asking about his physical strength: "Is it true, Mr Houdini, that you can resist

the hardest blows struck to the abdomen?" . . . It was in fact a surprising question. Nowhere in the available record does Houdini claim to be able to absorb punches to the stomach, although such a story may have gotten around along with much other spurious Houdini lore. Houdini . . . tried to divert attention away from his abdominal muscles by having the student feel his forearm and back muscles instead. His dodge did not satisfy Whitehead, however, who asked again if it was true that his stomach could withstand very hard blows. When Houdini again referred to the strength of his arms and back, Whitehead asked, "Would you mind if I delivered a few blows to your abdomen, Mr Houdini?"

Houdini accepted the challenge, as he had so many others. . . .

Whitehead's bizarre courtesy was matched by Houdini's eagerness to please. Eleven days later Houdini was dead of peritonitis, having suffured a ruptured appendix. It is impossible to know where the student had got the idea that Houdini would be prepared to rise to this particular challenge. But in this almost too emblematic scene—of youth against age, of the student against the uneducated rabbi's son, of the intellectual demand turning into a physical demand—the student did know that Houdini had some fundamental beliefs about the resilience of his body, and he knew Houdini's reputation as the man who met every challenge, who was interested in the possibilities of satisfying the most imperious of demands. Houdini had always allowed people—invited people—to handcuff him, to tie him up, to lock him in.

But the challenge had been imposed by the object. There was always something between him and the people testing him. With the aid of these objects, Houdini could use his remarkable skills as a mystifier. But there was no illusion to be mastered when he was repeatedly punched; there was only, quite literally, his body. If Houdini had always boasted that he was only human—and therefore must be an especially remarkable person—Whitehead exposed, at an elemental level, what being only human actually meant. Houdini didn't devise, but he did agree to, this final test. There was, he insisted, no magic, only illusion. The student, wittingly or unwittingly, revealed the limits of illusion. Apparently Houdini's last words were "I can't fight any more."

Perhaps one can define the times, and the individual people who live through them, by their exits; by what they think of themselves as having to escape from, and to confront, in order to have the lives they want. All modern people have their own repertoire of elsewheres, of alternatives—the places they go to in their minds, and the ambitions they attempt to realize—to make their actual, lived lives more than bearable. Indeed the whole notion of escape, that it is possible and desirable, is like a prosthetic device of the imagination. How could we live without it? And yet, of course, we are all equally mired in our immediate circumstances. It is these very circumstances that are productive of our alternative lives. The escape artist is always involved in some profound acknowledgment of just what it is she feels confined by. Her apprehension is exact and exacting.

All illusions, as Houdini called them, are realistic

accounts of something; even so-called delusions are exaggerated documentaries. Houdini's mock-suicides, his
staged traps, and his pronounced and pronouncing self-
advertisement, were signs of the times. Entertainment now
was the only available mass form of cultural thought-
fulness, at its most telling when it least intended to effect
any kind of change. Houdini the escape artist had more
to say—through his stunts—than Houdini the social
reformer, exposing spiritualists. What Houdini had to tell
pales in comparison with what Houdini had to show (just
as dream interpretations can be more ingeniously informative than dreams, but are rarely as evocative). Houdini, like Chaplin during and after him, was a cartoon
character for the times, and indeed, the precursor of the
cartoon escape artists Tom and Jerry, who could take all
the punches life gave them and whose lives came in
blows. In his wish to provide what his audience wanted—
to sustain its interest—he revealed, as all performers do,
something about the nature of that wanting (did the
student want to kill Houdini or reassure himself that
he couldn't?). In his insistence on man-made illusion
rather than divine magic, he was showing his audience,
knowingly or unknowingly, that wants are as man- and
woman-made as anything else. By offering himself up as a
hero (a "stage idol"), he was thrilling people with a testing of their ideals for themselves. Is it heroic just to be
able to escape? And is there something absurd, something
terrifying about the fact that what there is to escape from
is very often actually and ingeniously constructed by
oneself? If there is professional mystifying, there could

be, as the arc of Houdini's career illustrates, professional demystifying.

The question becomes—and Houdini's life dramatically asks and answers the question—what are we being encouraged to be impressed by, and by whom? Every moralist—which means every person—has his own story about moral options. The bad options are usually called escapist, the good options are usually called ideals. To keep them apart—to keep them as separate as we would wish them to be—often requires what Houdini called "mystifying." After all, we have made these distinctions, so we know we have the power to unmake them.

WHEN THE POET Emily Dickinson died in 1886 at the age of fifty-five, most of her neighbors hadn't seen her for well over twenty years. Withdrawing into her room in the family house at Amherst in the 1860s—"Friend, you thought / No life so sweet and fair as hiding brought," a friend, Emily Ford, wrote in a commemorative poem—she was only ever seen again by her immediate family. She was, in her own words, a "wayward Nun"—in local legend known as the Nun of Amherst—and even when old friends visited she would usually not make an appearance, sending a token gift downstairs instead, like a note or a flower. Such behavior then, as now, was considered to be rather strange; only the ill, the religious, and the criminal (and the criminally insane) tended to live in solitary confinement. Whether it was a vocation or an obscure punishment, her notorious seclusion became a kind of local spectacle. She so vividly disappeared from view, so eagerly confined herself in her room, that people couldn't help but speculate, both before and after her death, about just why she might have done it. Eccentricity has to be named; it has to have a cause and a reason and, ideally, a discernible purpose. In the religious battle between faith and sin, or the secular war between the plan and the accident, she must, people thought, have a plan. She must be either hiding or seeking. After all, what does a wayward nun want from life?

Her "gradual withdrawal," her friend Millicent Todd Bingham wrote, "was a natural response—given her genius—which she could have made to a world in which, as she said, there was so much matter-of-fact." Since the early nineteenth century it had become part of the ideology of genius, of the modern artist—conceived of as an unholy alliance of the religious, the criminal, and the insane—that he (and rarely she) would be essentially solitary. It was a sign of genius to be somehow disaffected with the matter-of-fact, not satisfied by, or even capable of, the ordinary genialities or the regular jobs. Whether, as her brother Austin thought, she had retreated because she wasn't beautiful, or whether, as many people thought, she had been wounded in love—there had been at least two unconsummated, possibly unbroached passions in her early life—Emily Dickinson didn't fit herself in, at least through the conventional channels of marriage and unofficial social work that constituted the lives of many women of her generation. She was determinedly unseen—all but a few of her startling, abundant poems were unpublished in her lifetime. It was interestingly unclear to her contemporaries, as it is to us, whether her early retirement was a sign of refusal or incapacity, in what sense it was chosen or she felt chosen for it. But narrowing the range of her life did not narrow her mind. Her self-imposed constraint liberated her. Like the apparently sparse staccato lines of her poems, she made her hidden life peculiarly resonant; it was a life that could only be full in the absence of too much recognition, and in the freedom from events. To carry off such a life—a life so starkly unmodern because it craved no publicity—required a kind of heroic tact.

The obituary written by her close friend and sister-in-law Susan Gilbert, published in the *Springfield Republican,* manages to capture in a remarkable way Dickinson's inspired and inspiring oddity. "Very few in the village," she wrote,

> except among the older inhabitants, knew miss Emily personally, although the facts of her seclusion and intellectual brilliancy were familiar Amherst traditions. . . . As she passed on in life, her sensitive nature shrank from much personal contact with the world, and more and more turned to her own large wealth of individual resources for companionship, sitting thenceforth, as someone said of her, "in the light of her own fire." Not dissappointed with the world, not an invalid until within the past two years, not from any lack of sympathy, not because she was insufficient for any

mental work or social career—her endowments being so exceptional—but the "mesh of her soul," as Browning calls the body, was too rare, and the sacred quiet of her own home proved the fit atmosphere for her worth and work. All that must be inviolate. One can only speak of "duties beautifully done"; of her gentle tillage of the rare flowers filling her conservatory, into which, as into the heavenly Paradise, entered nothing that could defile, and which was ever abloom in frost or sunshine, so well she knew her chemistries. . . . her talk and her writing were like no-one else's. . . . "Her wagon was hitched to a star,"— and who could ride or write with such a voyager? A Damascus blade gleaming and glancing in the sun was her wit. . . . quick as the lightning in her intuitions and analyses, she seized the kernel instantly, almost impatient of the fewest words, by which she must make her revelation.

It is an eloquent picture of an extremely purposeful and mysteriously resourceful life; as though she had a sense—"she knew her chemistries"—that the powers within her needed this seclusion. Her life was more an acknowledgment of her nature—of what she needed to do to be the person she believed herself to be—than a series of compensatory gestures for a felt inadequacy. However idealized this portrait is, or indeed her image of herself was, the unaccompanied life she sought and the purifications it entailed were as much a courting of danger as an evasion of it. Indeed, one of the dangers she so eloquently and incisively meditated in her poetry was

solitude itself. The perils and ecstasies of withdrawal—
whether they brought her closer to God or to the fraught
vacancies within herself, whether she could only love
people, including herself, in their absence—were her
theme. Confrontation was her continual subject, but her
revelation depended on her achieved solitude.

It is therefore of some interest that in a final quota of
over 1,700 poems she wrote two quite explicitly about
escape. And they are, in a sense, before-and-after poems:
the first probably written in 1860 before her seclusion had,
as it were, set in, and the second in 1875, ten years before
she died. Both poems pay tribute to the word itself. But
they celebrate its necessity in quite different ways. At the
age of thirty, she wrote:

> I never hear the word "Escape"
> Without a quicker blood,
> A sudden expectation—
> A flying attitude!
>
> I never hear of prisons broad
> By soldiers battered down,
> But I tug childish at my bars
> Only to fail again!

In the first verse there is an exhilaration and a readi-
ness in the word; but it's notably when she hears it from
someone else that her anticipation starts up. And now
that we, the readers, have heard it from her, we too are
expecting something. But once the poet is inspired by the
word she is diminished by the consequences; the whole

idea of escape merely reinforces her sense of helpless imprisonment (children, of course, unlike adults, are the people who can't choose to leave). Hearing of people abroad liberated by these soldiers—whether they are revolutionary soldiers or soldiers of Christ, and whether or not this casts the poet as a criminal or someone unjustly held— makes the poet want to liberate herself; and so once again to realize how little she can do. The idea of escape, however enlivening as a prospect, merely convinces her of her limitations. There is, she seems to say, no freedom in the notion of escape; it merely reveals what the prison is really like. Perhaps the poem intimates that she's waiting for a man, one of those soldiers, to liberate her, and the frustration, the resentment, is that she can't do it for herself. Whatever the possibilities, the word is a false promise, but the poem acknowledges the exhilaration of that promise. It doesn't need to play down the excitement that comes each time the word is heard. What would it be like, she makes us wonder, to live in a world without that word, and without stories about it? It is, she pointedly concludes the poem, failure, not success, to be so imprisoned.

In the second poem, written fifteen years later when Dickinson was forty-five, the poet is interestingly even more convinced of the value of this word, of what it consoles in us, and of the inspiration there is in comfort:

> Escape is such a thankful word
> I often in the Night
> Consider it unto myself
> No spectacle in sight

Escape—it is the Basket
In which the Heart is caught
When down some awful Battlement
The rest of Life is dropt—

'Tis not to sight the savior—
It is to be the saved—
And that is why I lay my head
Upon this trusty word—

Escape as a thankful word both makes one grateful
and gives thanks itself that we can imagine alternatives
for ourselves. It is not merely a hope (" 'Tis not to sight
the savior")—or a false hope, as the earlier poem claims—
it is itself, as a word, our redeeming feature. It is language
that both gives us heart—the word and all it suggests—
and stops us from falling (with all that that suggests).
Escape is a possibility made in language. Because it is
escape she is praising (if not hymning), she doesn't need
to tell us exactly what she is besieged by; whatever it is
in the night that persecutes her is no match for the basket, for all that single word holds and protects. Whether
it is a pillow for the saved or the damned—and the poem
is peculiarly transgressive in its favoring this particular
word over the word of God, or by even suggesting that
escape might be the word of God—this trusty word is the
final comfort of the visionary poet. Dickinson's lived life
had made the word trusty for her, she had proved it against
her darkest nights. It is a word whose services are no less
urgent now.

If it is the idea of escape—the mere word itself—that releases us from something, then language is complicit with our need to be able at least to imagine ourselves elsewhere. "Really alone at a real frontier," the poet Susan Howe wrote of Dickinson, "dwelling in Possibility was what she had brilliantly learned to do." And dwelling in possibility was as much dwelling in language as it was dwelling in her own room in her family house. It is, after all, in language that we can escape, whatever we then go on to do with our words ("Candor—my Preceptor—is the only wile," Dickinson wrote in a letter). It is as though, in both poems, Dickinson acknowledges that whatever it is that we must escape from, and whatever we believe we can escape to, the word is a necessity. It quickens us, a "trusty word" that helps us put our ambiguous trust in words.

In 1891, five years after her death, Thomas Wentworth Higginson described his first meeting with her in the *Atlantic Monthly*. His account is an emblem of a way of treating others, a tribute to someone who could call up such words in him, and an acknowledgment of Dickinson as a natural escape artist:

> She was much too enigmatical a being for me to solve in an hour's interview, and an instinct told me that the slightest attempt at direct cross-examination would make her withdraw into her shell; I could only sit and watch, as one does in the woods; I must name my bird without a gun, as recommended by Emerson.

ACKNOWLEDGMENTS

I RELIED ON Jane Brodie, Fiona Shaw, Sarah Spankie, Geoffrey Weaver, and Kate Weaver as my first readers. Without them I wouldn't have been able to see through the book, or see the book through. My agent (and friend) Felicity Rubenstein was, as ever, a prompt, close, and illuminating reader of the book at its various stages. Dan Frank's editing at Pantheon was inspired and inspiring.

Jacqueline Rose and Mia Rose provided the conditions without which this—and most of my other books—could never have been written.

Clive Panto, in over thirty years of friendship, has shown me among other things what it is to be interested in magic.

BIBLIOGRAPHY

Michael Balint, *Thrills and Regressions* (New York: International
    Universities Press, 1959).

Emily Dickinson, *The Poems of Emily Dickinson,* Variorum Edition,
    edited by R. W. Franklin (Cambridge, Mass.: Harvard Uni-
    versity Press, 1998).

Emily Dickinson, *Selected Letters,* edited by Thomas H. Johnson
    (Cambridge, Mass.: Harvard University Press, 1971).

Judith Farr, *The Passion of Emily Dickinson* (Cambridge, Mass.: Har-
    vard University Press, 1992).

Sándor Ferenczi, *First Contributions to Psychoanalysis,* translated by
    Ernest Jones (London: Hogarth Press, 1952).

Susan Howe, *My Emily Dickinson* (Berkeley, Calif.: North Atlan-
    tic Books, 1985).

Kenneth Silverman, *HOUDINI !!!, The Career of Ehrich Weiss* (New
    York: HarperCollins, 1996).

ABOUT THE AUTHOR

ADAM PHILLIPS is the author of *Winnicott; On Kissing, Tickling, and Being Bored; On Flirtation; Terror and Experts; Monogamy; The Beast in the Nursery; Darwin's Worms;* and *Promises, Promises.* Formerly the principal child psychotherapist at Charing Cross Hospital in London, he lives in England.